The Father's Heart in Flowers

Book 2

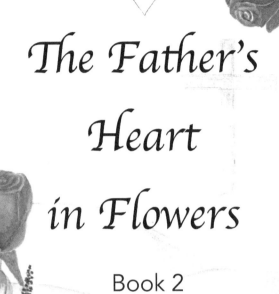

malcolm down

PUBLISHING

British Library Cataloguing in Publication Data
A catalogue record for this book is available from the British Library.

ISBN 978-1-915046-85-7

Cover design by Esther Kotecha
Art direction by Sarah Grace

Printed in the UK

Endorsements

We want to highly commend Margaret's latest offering *The Father's Heart in Flowers Book 2*.

Margaret expresses her love for Jesus, our Messiah, by using her excellent artistic gifts to show us how the seven annual Feasts of the Lord demonstrate the unfolding work of redemption through God's Son.

Jesus, as a Jew, would have observed and celebrated the Feasts (Hebrew *Moedim* – God's appointed times). The stories Margaret paints outline God's plan of salvation through the life, death, resurrection and return of Jesus Himself.

Margaret's exquisite paintings enable her to use her love of flowers to express the main ideas within each of the Feasts, as well as some important themes found in the scriptures.

Margaret's paintings are a joy to behold and have been beautifully woven into the text to produce a work that informs, enlightens and inspires the reader.

Aggy and Sue

Margaret Brewer and her husband Geoff have been our special friends for many years.

Margaret has many talents that she has nurtured and grown and is using to spread the wonderful Word of God, the Bible, to all who will read her work. She has not hidden her many artistic giftings, such as botanical illustration and painting or the lovely gift of flower arranging, and with Geoff's help the writing of the Bible stories and the words of Jesus. Margaret is letting her light shine out for all to see (Matthew 5:14-16). A magnificent way to spread the gospel. Margaret and Geoff both have a love of wildlife, trees, grasses, flowers, fields and hedgerows, birds, bees and butterflies. They both adore God's amazing creation.

As we read Margaret's books we are reminded of Mrs Alexander's hymn:

All things bright and beautiful.
All creatures great and small,
All things wise and wonderful,
The Lord God made them all.

Derek and Rita Harrison

It is an honour to write this endorsement for my friend Margaret. There are four chapters within this book that resonate with me. These four chapters pertaining to God's *Moedim*, His appointed Feasts: Passover, Unleavened Bread, Firstfruits, Shavuot/Pentecost, Rosh Hashanah/Feast of Trumpets. Yom Kippur/Feast of Atonement, Sukkot/Feast of Tabernacles.

I found these chapters to be a breath of fresh air, insightful and engaging. This is a book for everyone, easy to read and easy to understand. The expressions used to outline these biblical Feasts have been made very clear. These chapters are informative and inclusive of new believers in Jesus/Yeshua, our Jewish Messiah.

From the onset of reading these chapters I felt the Holy Spirit's presence on every page. God was unlocking my heart and drawing me into a closer relationship with Him. I could only imagine that this would have the same impact on all who read this book.

Margaret has clearly listened, understood and captured God's heart for the salvation of mankind through the lens of His *Moedim*. I would say He has given Margaret vivid vision on how to execute this side-by-side revelation on how to simplify what was first covenant promises whilst illustrating fulfilment through the Spring Feasts, Passover, Unleavened Bread, Firstfruits and Shavuot/Pentecost. God does not want His church to be ignorant or lack knowledge and understanding in His Word, hence why Margaret has captured and highlighted the passion in God's heart within these four chapters.

She has used a simpler way of communicating God's heart and hopefully should arouse greater awareness that God's Word is about seed time and harvest based on an agricultural calendar by looking at it through 'His eye's lens' bringing fulfilment to Bible prophecy.

I am able to appreciate Margaret's intention to prevent readers from teachings that could hinder the flow of revelation and understanding that has circulated over many decades.

This book would be incomplete if Margaret hadn't captured Paul's understanding of Romans 11. God's olive tree, clearly portrayed in scripture as being Israel. They are the natural branches and Gentiles (church believers) are the wild cultivated olive branches that are grafted to make a full tree.

Yeshua/Jesus has instructed us to not boast or to dishonour Israel in any way because we (Gentiles) can be cut from the tree and no longer be included. However, it is God's desire to make us one. The olive tree is uniquely called to bear fruit together, this is a wonderful illustration of the One New Man, the Body of Christ/Yeshua, the Bride of Christ.

Thank you, Margaret, for delivering in-depth knowledge and revelation in a straightforward way.

The Lord has truly gifted Margaret 'the tongue of a ready writer' (Psalm 45:1).

Annette Powell
Echad Ministries

First and foremost, I would like to thank my husband, Geoff, without whom this book would not have been written. Over the years he has not only helped me with making the accessories needed for my arrangements, but he has also typed out the messages for this book. He gives me loving advice and encouragement whenever it has been needed.

I would also like to say a big thank you to two of my grandchildren, Matthew and his sister Naomi. When I have required help in putting the text and illustrations together on the laptop their knowledge and expertise have been invaluable.

Matthew is an accomplished artist in his own right. He painted the 'Alpha and Omega' and the 'Lion and Lamb' on pages 178 and 190 respectively. My ability to paint is only in the realm of 'Botanical Art'.

My thanks must also go to local artist, Liz Cosh, for allowing me to include her truly inspirational and beautiful card Apple of God's Eye, which you can see in 'The Olive Tree' on page 55.

I would like to thank our dear long-time friends Derek and Rita who looked at the finished work for me, Aggy and Sue for checking the text for grammatical correctness and scriptural content. To Annette and her husband's work in Echad Ministries, for opening my eyes to the relevance of Israel, found in the 'Feasts given to Moses' many years ago, pointing to God's plan of redemption and the oneness between Jew and Gentile (see The Olive Tree).

A special thank you to our paster Martin Ceaser for writing the Foreword. He and his wife Ali are a constant source of love and encouragement. Ali also introduced me to the publisher, so my thanks go to Malcolm Down and Sarah Grace Publishing for agreeing to publish this book for me.

I would also like to say a special thank you to all my family, for their love, support and encouragement.

Last but certainly not least, I thank the God of Israel Who has blessed each one of us with His eternal gift of salvation through His Son Jesus and for the gift of His Holy Spirit. May our hearts and voices always sing His praises.

Margaret Brewer has lived her whole life in Bedfordshire; John Bunyan's county, as she calls it. She and her husband have four children, eight grandchildren and two great-grandchildren. A daughter of a Methodist lay preacher, her Christian faith is central to her life.

Margaret's three greatest passions are faith, family and flowers. She has always loved flowers: growing them, arranging them and more recently painting them. Since retiring from work as a nursing assistant at a day hospital she has studied with The Society of Botanic Artists and passed with credit, has a City and Guilds in Flower Arranging and won a silver medal at the Chelsea Flower Show. Over the years she has incorporated a Christian message with floral arrangement demonstrations. An idea began forming to write down her messages illustrated by paintings of the flower arrangements, which has then developed into two books.

Margaret continues to worship at a local Baptist church and, along with her husband, helps to run a midweek fellowship afternoon.

Contents

Margaret Brewer is a miracle worker – she takes flowers and turns them into stunningly beautiful illustrations of Bible stories, colourful combinations that point to Jesus and speak powerfully into the lives of anyone who sets eyes on them. That's the main miracle, but there's another – she has made someone who has never really appreciated flowers in church see that in the right hands they have a big role to play. She has the gift of being able to interpret the essence of the biblical account and represent it with her arrangements, and I am very grateful to her for opening the eyes of this middle-aged minister in this way!

As if that were not enough Margaret has a gift with words, which she uses to great effect in this book, explaining the importance of the passages and references that the flowers refer to. Here, she carefully explores and explains the major festivals of the Old Testament in the light of the life, death and resurrection of Jesus – and in particular how each festival is a prophetic enactment foreshadowing the promised Messiah. Her love for Jesus, for the Scriptures, for the Jewish people and of course for flowers, shines through in each chapter and can, if we let them, point us to Christ and help us deepen our relationship with Him.

This is a book that can be read right through in a couple of sittings, or it can be read more slowly, devotionally, or even as a study for individuals and small groups. It would make a great gift for people of faith or no faith, and Margaret's beautiful illustrations make it an excellent choice for a 'coffee table' book.

In Matthew's Gospel, chapter 6 verses 28-31, Jesus says, **'See how the lilies of the field grow. They do not labour or spin. Yet I tell you that not even Solomon in all his splendour was dressed like one of these. If that is how God clothes the grass of the field, which is here today and tomorrow is thrown into the fire, will he not much more clothe you, O you of little faith?'** In this book Margaret takes us on a journey of considering the lilies (flowers), using them in conjunction with the Scriptures in a way that can and does show us just how precious we are to God; how because of that we can trust Him in every season of our lives; and that in Jesus we find the greatest beauty of all, the offer of forgiveness, grace and a relationship with God Himself.

May you know His blessing as you turn the pages of this book.

Reverend Martin Ceaser
Minister
Biggleswade Baptist Church

I have always appreciated the beauty of flowers, and loved watching as the demonstrator at our local flower club made beautiful designs using flowers. So a friend and I decided to enrol on a City and Guilds course in flower arranging. It was there I learned about interpretive work, in which you are given a title and you depict it in flowers. Which to me becomes floral art, because you are telling a story with flowers.

At about the same time in my Christian walk, see 'The Beginnings of a Pilgrim', I had what I call a 'Head to heart' moment. My head knowledge of God became heart knowledge, when I truly realised what God had done for me and each one of us through Jesus. I longed to tell others what I had found in Him but didn't know how! When a friend asked me to do a demonstration at a midweek fellowship meeting, so it started me thinking of how we can use interpretive flower designs to tell the gospel story, which I have been doing now for nearly thirty years, in local groups, both Christian and non Christian. The format consists of a short explanation of the title, followed by three floral art illustrations interspersed with the message, concluding with the summary.

My first book on the subject *The Fathers Heart in Flowers* came out in 2018. Then by 2020 the world had gone in to 'lockdown' because of a global pandemic.

It has been a strange and difficult time for many people. Some have spent a long time in hospital, some have lost loved ones. It has also had an impact on the world economy. Businesses and jobs have been affected. We don't always find answers to the things that trouble us. Paul tells us in Ephesians that we should put on 'The Armour of God,' replace our fears with faith.

Our God has given us the Scriptures, which contain advice for living, as well as many prophecies of things yet to come. So we have to trust in Him and His Word.

Because He is the . . .

'Alpha and Omega the Beginning and the end.' When the children of Israel were in the wilderness, God gave Moses 'Seven Feasts' that they were to keep. I was astounded when studying these to realise that these Seven Feasts point to God's plan of redemption, 1,500 years before Jesus was born. One last thought about 'The Wilderness Years'. It's estimated that the number of men, women and children to make the journey from Egypt to Succoth (Exodus 12:37-38) could easily have made 2 million, plus their livestock and belongings.

The responsibility that lay on the shoulders of Moses must have been horrendous. After the incident of the 'Golden Calf' (Exodus chapters 32–33) Moses went into the 'Tent of Meeting' to pray with Joshua. He asked God to forgive the people, then he began to doubt his call to leadership! Was God really with him? The Lord God tried to reassure him, but Moses needed more.

'Please, show me your glory.' 33:18

The Lord told him to go alone up the mountain and stand in the 'cleft of the rock'.

The Lord came to him in his isolation, fears and worries.

So when we are feeling alone, fearful and worried, draw near to Him and ask our 'gracious and compassionate' God to give you the assurance, that whatever happens He is always with us. Jesus said. . .

'Lo, I am with you always, even to the end of the age.'
Amen. Matthew 28:20.

The Beginnings

Of A

Pilgrim

Unfurling Dryopteris (male Fern)

One day our minister, after seeing me present a gospel message in flowers, asked me if I ever thought of doing my own testimony in flowers. This started me wondering how to express in flowers the joy of salvation and the wonderful times when the Holy Spirit shows you truths that previously you had not seen. That we have a holy and awesome God, who is the beginning and the end. Whose word is truth and everlasting. How can I illustrate that in flowers?

A few years previously I had read my grandad's copy of John Bunyan's *The Pilgrim's Progress*. It was printed in the year 1915. The book not only contains Christian's walk of faith but also his wife Christiana's. Although they encountered different people and had many doubts, fears and problems on their pilgrimage to reach the Celestial City, I noticed that three things were the same for both of them.

- Both went through the gate – Jesus.
- The Interpreter's House – both had an encounter with the Holy Spirit.
- Both went up the path that led them to the cross – where sins are dealt with and forgiveness is found.

So using those illustrations this is my attempt to give my testimony in flowers.

1st Arrangement: The Gate

*'I am the gate; whoever enters through
me will be saved.'*
John 10:9

*'Jesus said again, "Very truly I tell you, I am the gate for the sheep.
All who have come before me are thieves and robbers."'*
John 10:7-8

Christian, knowing the world is going the wrong way, sets out for the Celestial City. He encounters all sorts of situations and people on his journey. The first person he comes across is Evangelist who points him to the 'Gate'.

**The Gate is believing in Jesus and knowing we
come to the Father through Him.**

I was at the Gate for thirty-four years. I was brought up in a Christian home, my dad was a lay preacher. So, yes, I believed in Jesus. In my teenage years I went out with my friends enjoying youth clubs, dancing, etc. while still attending church on Sundays. I was in my thirties when I began to question and at times started to feel discouraged.

Christian would call it the 'Slough of Despond'.

A Christian friend had marriage problems, even though there was a lot of prayer for them there didn't seem to be a reconciliation. I began to wonder, if God could bring a whole nation out of slavery in Egypt, why couldn't He get those two people back together? Was the Bible still relevant in today's world?

Then my husband, Geoff, had back problems. He was being treated by the doctor but it just kept getting worse. I half joked to my new neighbour that I would have to find a faith healer. That evening her husband came round to see me and warned me about faith healing, saying when we pray for healing it should only be through Jesus. I had never heard anyone talk like this before, and we started talking about Christianity. I told him I had always been a Christian. His answer took me by surprise. He said, 'Look at it this way: you can sit in a garage all your life, it still won't make you into a car.' I felt a bit upset by what he had said, but at the same time I thought they had something I didn't. I knew of Jesus, but didn't know Him. I began to feel like a hypocrite.

Anyway, Geoff just got worse. He was taken into hospital. We were told he would never work as a plumber again, never paint the house or dig the garden. Our lives seemed to take a turn for the worse. We had four small children and a mortgage. How would we manage?

One day when I was visiting my husband in hospital I saw our minister. I told him about Geoff and he asked how I was coping. Still feeling a bit fed up I said, 'With a little help from my friends, thank you,' meaning, I don't need you or your church! Sometime later, when he heard Geoff was home, he came to see him. Before he left I shared with him how I was feeling: the doubts, that I felt like a hypocrite and if I didn't find something more I would have to leave the church. He was writing something down as I was speaking and gave it to me and then he left. He was pointing me to Christian's next point,

THE CROSS.

2nd Arrangement: The Cross

'"He himself bore our sins" in his body on the cross,
so that we might die to sins and live for righteousness.'
1 Peter 2:24

'Just as Christian came up to the cross, his burden loosed from off
his shoulders, and fell off his back, and began to tumble, and so
continued on till it came to the mouth of the sepulchre,
where it fell in and I saw it no more.'
The Pilgrim's Progress by John Bunyan

When Christian came through the gate his burden was still on his back. He asked Goodwill if he could help him off with his burden, but he was told, 'When you come to the place of deliverance it will just fall off.' When Christian came to the cross, that place of deliverance, his burden (his sin) rolled off his back.

I had been baptised as a baby, confirmed at thirteen, but still needed to come to the cross. The minister had written down six things for me:

- God wants you to have abundant life, as Jesus said in John chapter 10:10, in which you know Him as Saviour and Lord.

- The barrier to this is sin, and only Christ can take this away. Sin is falling short of what God wants you to be, and to do. Jesus broke the power of sin and evil on the cross.

- Look at ourselves in the light of Jesus and name the sins you can see. Confess them to Jesus and claim His forgiveness (1 John 1:8-9).

- Accept His forgiveness, not because of your feelings but because you have obeyed His Word. Hold within yourself the confidence that He has forgiven you.

- Offer God your whole life. He is concerned about every part, and can direct and help you with each day's duties. Tell Him you want to do His will as fully as you can.

Paeonia lactiflora.

So, in the quietness of my own room I thought of myself in the light of Jesus and found sins I hadn't seen before. So I confessed my sins to Him and asked Him to forgive me, and come into my life. I felt set free, forgiven, Jesus became real to me. I knew without a shadow of a doubt that it was all true, and just as relevant today as it was when the children of Israel were set free. Everyday problems were still there but He gives us peace and joy, He puts a new song in our hearts and gives us that blessed assurance.

3rd Arrangement: The Interpreter's House

'The Holy Spirit, whom the Father will send
in my name, will teach you all things and will
remind you of everything I have said to you.'
John 14:26

'When He, the Spirit of truth, has come, He will guide you into all truth;
for He will not speak on His own authority, but whatever He hears
He will speak; and He will tell you things to come. He will glorify Me,
for He will take of what is Mine and declare it to you.'
John 16:13-14 NKJV

The third major point John Bunyan shows us is that Christian goes to the Interpreter's House. The Interpreter, or Holy Spirit, revealed to him deep spiritual truths. He told him the law cannot save, only the gospel. He showed him things to come and told him the Comforter would always be with him to guide him on his way.

Tulip and Lunaria annua 'Honesty'

The sixth and last piece of advice the minister had been writing down for me was,

- Ask for the gift of the Holy Spirit. He is the source of power, confidence and all the gifts we need to serve God (John 14:15-17, Acts 1:8).

I didn't understand this, I knew the Holy Spirit was given to the disciples in the book of Acts, but I didn't realise that the gift of the Spirit is for today also and that every believer could receive the Holy Spirit. I guess I thought the Holy Spirit had just been given to certain people, like the disciples, who were called by God to do great things. Next time he came to see us I asked him, 'What is the Holy Spirit?' He said, 'I haven't time to explain it to you now, but basically it's what is happening to you already.' So once again, in the quietness of my room, I asked for the gift of the Holy Spirit. I had a very real assurance of His presence. My head and my heart were filled with praise. The words of the Lord's Prayer seemed to come on my mind like a branding iron. I couldn't sleep; just to bask in the joy of His presence was all I needed. My days were busy with the children but as I stood cooking or ironing the meaning of the parables and the things Jesus said would become clear to me. Head knowledge became heart knowledge. He continues to guide, comfort and teach.

Alstroemeria   'Peruvian Lily.

Most of us, whether we have been brought up in the church or not, feel we are decent law-abiding people. We haven't murdered anyone or robbed a bank or done anything really bad. So what is this about confessing our sins? Do we really have to do that?

It was the third point the minster gave me about looking at ourselves in the light of Jesus that spoke to me on this question of sin. When we really look at Him – how He lived, showing love, kindness and mercy to all people. Even when He was rejected, betrayed and crucified He held no bitterness or resentment, He just continued to love us. As He was nailed to that awful cross for the sins that we commit He said, 'Father, forgive them, for they do not know what they are doing' (Luke 23:34). Even if I am just treated unkindly, would I be able to forgive like that? It's not only His life but also His teaching. When I look at the Sermon on the Mount in Matthew chapters 5 to 7, can I really say I have never sinned? No, I couldn't say that, even in my high opinion of myself, I knew I could never be good enough. This is why He came.

John 3:16-18 says, 'God so loved the world that he gave his one and only Son, that whoever believes in him shall not perish but have eternal life. For God did not send his Son into the world to condemn the world, but to save the world through him. Whoever believes in him is not condemned, but whoever does not believe stands condemned already because they have not believed in the name of God's one and only Son.' Also, 1 John 1:8-9 says, 'If we claim to be without sin, we deceive ourselves and the truth is not in us. If we confess our sins, he is faithful and just and will forgive us our sins and purify us from all unrighteousness.'

The Lord touched each one of us in His own way. Geoff and each of our four children made a commitment to the Lord to follow and serve Him. And what happened to Geoff's back? He went forward for prayer at a Sunday evening service and the Lord placed His healing hand upon him. He continued in his job as a plumber for another thirty-two years until he retired. He still paints the house and digs the garden.

Praise His Holy Name.

If you are standing just inside 'The Gate' as I was, can I encourage you to keep going until you come to the 'Interpreter's House' to seek the gift of the Holy Spirit, and also that place of deliverance.

That Wonderful, Wonderful Cross.

Blessed assurance, Jesus is mine;
Oh, what a foretaste of glory divine!
Heir of salvation, purchase of God;
Born of His Spirit washed in His blood:

This is my story, this is my song,
Praising my Saviour all the day long.

Fanny J. Crosby
(1820–1915)

Mary
And
Elizabeth

One of my favourite Christmas songs, is 'Mary, Did You Know?' written by Mark Lowry and Buddy Greene. It tells of the miracles of Jesus, how He healed the sick, raised the dead and one day His life would bring deliverance to all people, including Mary. It poses the question: 'Mary, did you know?'

It started me thinking, how much did she know? How much did she understand what was happening to her? She must have known prophecies about the One who is to come, that God would send a Messiah to save His people.

The Bible gives no information about her parentage, only that she was a young girl living in Nazareth and engaged to a man called Joseph, who was in the line of David, going back via Judah to Abraham. The only clue we have is that Elizabeth's ancestry traces back to Aaron (Luke 1:5) and that Mary was a relative of Elizabeth. Some versions say cousin. So we will see how the lives of these 'cousins' are forever linked in God's plan to bring peace and salvation to His people.

Rose.
Myosotis, Forget-me-not.

1st Arrangement: The Angel Gabriel

'Therefore the Lord himself will give you a sign: the virgin will conceive and give birth to a son, and will call him Immanuel.'
Isaiah 7:14

'The angel [Gabriel] said to her, "Do not be afraid, Mary, you have found favour with God. You will conceive and give birth to a son, and you are to call him Jesus.'
Luke 1:30-31

One day the angel Gabriel came to Mary and told her not to be afraid, that she would conceive and give birth to a son. When she asked how that could happen as she was still a virgin, the angel answered saying that the Holy Spirit would come upon her and the power of the Most High overshadow her. The holy one to be born would be called the Son of God. She was to name Him Jesus.

Mary must have been bewildered and scared. If she accepted what God was asking of her she would be disgraced.

What would Joseph say?
Would he believe her when she told him what had happened?
Was it real or was it just a dream?

But she surrendered all her fears and anxieties and, in faith, accepted God's will for her life, saying, 'I am the Lord's servant . . . May your word to me be fulfilled' (Luke 1:38).

God understood her fear and sent the angel to Joseph also, explaining to him that what had happened to Mary was a fulfilment of a prophecy that 'the virgin will conceive and give birth to a son, and they will call him Immanuel (which means "God with us")' (Matthew 1:22-23). The angel also told Mary that Elizabeth, after years of being unable to conceive, was also with child.

Sprayed seedheads of   Nicandra physalodes, or Shoo-fly.

Mary decides to visit her in the hill country of Judea. The Bible tells us that when Elizabeth heard Mary's greeting, the baby leapt in her womb and Elizabeth, filled with the Holy Spirit, said,

'Blessed are you among women, and blessed
is the child you will bear!
But why am I so favoured,
that the mother of my Lord should come to me?'

Luke 1:42-43

At that Mary bursts into song, with praise and prophecy, which today we call the Magnificat.

'My soul glorifies the Lord and my spirit rejoices in God my Saviour . . .'

Luke 1:46-55

2nd Arrangement: **Two Women Forever Linked**

'Mary stayed with Elizabeth for about three months.'
Luke 1:56

Arrangement incorporating two body shapes linked together
by flowers and Midelino sticks.

Let us look for a moment at Elizabeth's pregnancy from the point of view of Zechariah, her husband. He was a priest serving God in Judea. They were getting on in years and still had no children. He must have prayed many times that the Lord would bless them with a child (Luke 1:5-25).

At the regular prayer times in the temple, the priest would also tend to the incense on the golden altar that stood in front of the Most Holy Place where the Ark of the Covenant was kept. One day it was his turn to burn the incense. All the assembled worshippers were praying outside as he went into the Holy Place to burn the incense. It was at that moment an angel of the Lord appeared to him and told him his prayers had been heard and his wife would bear a son, and they were to call him John. Because at first he didn't believe the angel, he was told he would be unable to speak until after his son was born. Eight days after the birth they went to the temple for the child to be circumcised and named. When he wrote on the writing tablet that his name was to be John, immediately his mouth was opened and his tongue set free. Filled with the Holy Spirit he began praising and prophesying.

'Praise be to the Lord, the God of Israel, because he has come to his people and redeemed them ...'
[Then addressing John] 'And you, my child, will be called a prophet of the Most High; for you will go on before the Lord to prepare the way for him, to give his people the knowledge of salvation through the forgiveness of their sins ...'
Luke 1:68-79

That's exactly what John did. He was the one who prepared the way for his and our Lord and Saviour.

Three months later Jesus was born. When He was taken to the temple on the eighth day, Simeon, the priest, recognised this small baby as the promised Messiah. He also told Mary,

'A sword will pierce your own soul.'
Luke 2:35

3rd Arrangement: A Sword Would Pierce Her Soul

'Then Simeon blessed them and said to Mary . . .
"And a sword will pierce your own soul . . ."'
Luke 2:34-35

Incorporating a heart, teardrop-shaped baubles and
Phormium tenax leaves, dried and sprayed silver,
representing the sword.

We don't know if Joseph, Zechariah or Elizabeth were there when the time came for both their sons to face a horrific death, but Mary certainly was. She faced many trials. Soon after she gave birth to Jesus she and Joseph had to flee to Egypt when Satan, through Herod, tried to destroy the work of God at the onset by killing all the baby boys in the area under two.

After her initial fears, when He started His ministry, she supported Him all the way (Mark 3:20-21, 31-34).

She was there when He healed the sick,
Raised the dead,
Drove out demons.

She was there when He was arrested,
Tried,
Stripped,
Whipped,
Spat on,
Mocked,
A crown of thorns pushed on His head
And CRUCIFIED.

The sword that pieced His side,
Must have also pieced her innermost being,
Her soul.

Scindapsus aureus. or Devil's Ivy.

35

Hippeastrum
or Amaryllis.

When we think of the Christmas story our thoughts go to the nativity scene that our children love to act out for us, and which we all love to watch. However, this is not just about a physical birth, but a spiritual birth, of the kingdom of God on earth. That came in dynamic power.

For hundreds of years the voice of prophecy had been silent, but suddenly prophecies are about to be fulfilled. God comes to earth in the form of a baby. An angel came to Joseph in a dream and opened his eyes to the prophecy in Isaiah! Elizabeth, filled with the Holy Spirit, realised the baby Mary was carrying was her Lord! Zechariah's praise is filled with the realisation of prophecy fulfilled as well as a prophetic word for the future. That's without mentioning Simeon and Anna or angel voices as they drift from the heavenly realm into the physical giving praise and proclamation to His coming!!

Mary stayed faithful to her God and Saviour to the very end. She was there in the upper room when the Holy Spirit came upon them.

As we come to know Jesus, we grow in the knowledge of God, with the Holy Spirit revealing truths to us when we are ready to receive and accept.

In that moment when Mary heard Elizabeth's reply to her greeting and burst into song, I believe she experienced what I call a 'head to heart' moment.

Yes! She believed in God.
Yes! She had said yes to His will in her life.
But! In that moment, the veil dropped from her eyes
as she realised it was all true.
Her head knowledge became heart knowledge.
But did she fully understand what was happening?

'Mary, did you know?'

I will leave you to answer that one.

Ornithogalum umbellatum or 'Star of Bethlehem'.

37

'Near the cross of Jesus stood his mother ... When
Jesus saw his mother there, and the disciple
whom he loved standing nearby, he said to her,
"Woman, here is your son," and to the disciple,
"Here is your mother." From that time on,
this disciple took her into his home.'

John 19:25-27

Even as He was dying, Jesus was showing
love and concern for His mother.

Joseph's Storehouse

Is

'His-story'

Bergenia cordifolia

Joseph lived approximately two thousand years before Jesus was born, yet, when I was reading the story of his life in Genesis chapters 37 to 47, I was astounded how his life reflects the life of Jesus. A few days later I was sharing my thoughts with a friend who lent me a book from the 1920s called *The Study of the Types* by Ada Habershon.

In her study of Joseph she lists approximately one hundred and fifty-three references as a type of Christ.

Jesus often refers to the happenings in the Old Testament and in a spiritual sense likens them to Himself.

Also, when asked for a sign from the Scribes and the Pharisees, Jesus said, 'None will be given . . . except the sign of the prophet Jonah. For as Jonah was three days and three nights in the belly of a huge fish, so the Son of Man will be three days and three nights in the heart of the earth' (Matthew 12:39-40).

In Luke 18:31-34 He explained to His disciples that He would be put to death and He would rise again on the third day.

Also Manna from heaven – He is our spiritual food.
The bronze snake – we come to Him to be made whole.

So let us look at the life of Joseph and see
how it reflects

'His-story'.

Phlomis
Seed head.

Lysimachia.

Joseph's father, Jacob, was the son of Isaac and the grandson of Abraham. The Bible tells us that at one stage in his life Jacob 'wrestled' with God and God said to him, 'Your name will no longer be Jacob, but Israel' (Genesis 32:22-30).

We take up the story again in Genesis chapter 37 when Jacob (or Israel) was living in Canaan with his twelve sons. They were shepherds.

Jesus said, 'I am the good shepherd' (John 10:11).

Please note that in this story of Joseph, references to Jesus are in red.

1st Arrangement: The Blood-soaked Robe

'Then they got Joseph's robe, slaughtered
a goat and dipped the robe in the blood.'
Genesis 37:31

Incorporating a metal cowl sprayed brown/black to indicate earth and
placed upside down with flowers arranged inside to indicate a pit.
A red cloth flowing from inside the container for the blood-soaked robe.
Flowers arranged in and around the sides.

When Joseph was seventeen he had two strange dreams. The first was that he and his brothers were binding sheaves of corn, when suddenly his sheave rose up and his brothers' sheaves gathered round and bowed down to it. The second dream was that the sun, moon and eleven stars were bowing down to him (Genesis chapter 37).

His father kept what he said in mind (v11).

The mother of Jesus 'treasured all these things in her heart' (Luke 2:51).

But . . . his brothers, when they saw how much their father loved him, and what his dreams were implying, hated him (v4).

Jesus said, 'They hated me without reason' (John 15:25).

One day Joseph's father sent him to see if all was well with his brothers (v14).

Jesus said, 'I was sent only to the lost sheep of Israel' (Matthew 15:24).

When Joseph's brothers saw him coming, they plotted to kill him (v18).

'The chief priests and the elders . . . made their plans how to have Jesus executed' (Matthew 27:1).

They stripped Joseph of his robe (v23).

'They stripped [Jesus] and put a scarlet robe on him' (Matthew 27:28).

But, instead of killing Joseph they sold him for twenty pieces of silver (v28).

Jesus was sold for thirty pieces of silver (Matthew 26:15).

Joseph was taken to Egypt (v36).

As a baby Jesus was taken into Egypt because Herod wanted to kill Him . . . 'Out of Egypt I called my son' (Matthew 2:14-15).

Then Joseph's brothers killed a goat and dipped his robe in its blood (v31). They tried to cover their sin with the blood.

At the trial of Jesus the people said, 'His blood is upon us' (Matthew 27:25).

Diaenira spectabilis.   'Bleeding Heart.'

The Blood-soaked Robe

Joseph's brothers had planned to kill him but sold him instead. To cover up their crime they killed a goat and dipped his robe in its blood and let their father believe that Joseph had been killed by a wild animal. Instead, they sold him to Midianite merchants who took him to Egypt to be sold as a slave. Joseph must have felt very alone.

Just as the Father was with Jesus, Genesis 39:2 says, 'The LORD was with Joseph.'

> Jesus said, 'I am not alone, for my Father is with me' (John 16:32).

Joseph was bought by Potiphar, one of Pharaoh's officials, who put him in charge of his household and all that he owned. The Lord blessed Potiphar because of Joseph (v5).

> Our heavenly Father has placed everything in the hands of Jesus, and He has blessed us with every spiritual blessing.

2nd Arrangement: The Prison and the Cross

'Joseph's master took him and put him in prison.'
Genesis 39:20

*'They brought Jesus to the place called Golgotha ...
And they crucified him.'*
Mark 15:22-24

Incorporating a cross with bread (to represent the baker) on one side and grapes on the other (to represent the cup bearer). Under the bread is the prison or tomb (e.g. made from a raffia lampshade with some raffia cut out then sprayed black and purple), with one lily head placed inside indicating death; the arrangement under grapes indicates life.

All was going well for Joseph. Potiphar could see that the Lord was with him so his trust in him grew. He put him in charge of his household and everything he owned. Until Potiphar's wife accused him of something he didn't do and he was put in prison (Genesis 39:19-20).

Both Jesus and Joseph were wrongly accused, bound and held as prisoners. With Joseph in prison were two of Pharaoh's officials: his chief cupbearer and his chief baker. When interpreting their dreams Joseph told them one would die and one would live.

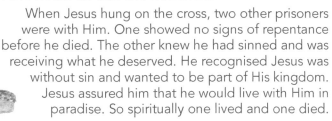

When Jesus hung on the cross, two other prisoners were with Him. One showed no signs of repentance before he died. The other knew he had sinned and was receiving what he deserved. He recognised Jesus was without sin and wanted to be part of His kingdom. Jesus assured him that he would live with Him in paradise. So spiritually one lived and one died.

Jesus returned to the Father, until the appointed time of His return.

Joseph was released from prison when Pharaoh wanted some dreams interpreted and his cupbearer remembered what Joseph had done for him (Genesis 41). Joseph told Pharaoh there would be seven years of abundance in the harvest, and seven years of famine. Pharaoh asked them, 'Can we find anyone like this man, one in whom is the spirit of God? . . . There is no one so discerning and wise as you' (Genesis 41:38-39).

Isn't that what we think of Jesus, can we find anyone else like Him?

Pharaoh said to Joseph, 'You shall be over my house, and all my people shall be ruled according to your word; only in regard to the throne will I be greater than you' (v40 NKJV).

'Christ is faithful as the Son over God's house' (Hebrews 3:6). Jesus said, 'I do nothing on my own but speak just what the Father has taught me' (John 8:28).

Joseph was thirty years old when he entered the service of Pharaoh the king (v46).

Jesus was about thirty years old when He started His ministry (Luke 3:23).

Seven years of abundance came to an end. And seven years of famine began. When the people cried to Pharaoh, he said, 'Go to Joseph; whatever he says to you, do' (v55 NKJV).

Peter answered, 'Lord, to whom shall we go? You have the words of eternal life' (John 6:68 NKJV). Jesus's mother said, 'Do whatever he tells you' (John 2:5).

Joseph opened the storehouses and people came from every country to buy grain (v56-57).

Of Jesus it is said, 'He who supplies seed to the sower and bread for food . . . will enlarge the harvest of your righteousness' (2 Corinthians 9:10).

3rd Arrangement: **Treasure in Their Sacks**

'Those of my own race, the people of Israel. Theirs is adoption to sonship; theirs the divine glory, the covenants, the receiving of the law, the temple worship and the promises. Theirs are the patriarchs, and from them is traced the human ancestry of the Messiah, who is God over all, for ever praised! Amen.

Romans 9:3-5

Incorporating corn stack container made by fixing two plant pots together then covering in corn, with flowers arranged in the centre. Two purple net sacks filled with grain and gold (e.g. painted avocado stones) for the treasure.

Then we come to that wonderful part of the story where Joseph and his brothers are reconciled and Joseph's dreams are about to be fulfilled (Genesis 42).

As the famine intensified, ten of Joseph's brothers came to buy grain. They didn't recognise him, but as they bowed down before him Joseph recognised them. He concocted a plan, not in spite but so he could see his younger brother, Benjamin. Joseph, not wanting to be recognised, talked to them through an interpreter.

> We have an interpreter who interprets the Word of God to us.
> The Holy Spirit (John 16:13-15).

Joseph said they could take some grain back to their father and families, but when they returned they were to bring Benjamin with them. Joseph insisted that they were to leave one brother as a hostage. Joseph gave orders to fill their sacks with grain, to put their money back in their sacks and to give them provision for the journey.

> Two scriptures relate: We cannot buy the kingdom of God (Isaiah 55:1)
> and He will meet all our needs (Philippians 4:19).

When they returned with Benjamin, they were worried about the money that was put back in their sacks. But Joseph's steward said to them, 'Don't be afraid. Your God, the God of your father, has given you treasure in your sacks' (Genesis 43:18-23).

What is the treasure? Over the years that 'gold' became adoption of sonship, divine glory, the covenants, the law, the temple worship, the promises, the patriarchs and the human ancestry of the Messiah.

This story not only foreshadows Jesus's life on earth and is relevant for us today, but also spills over into the future. Just as the sons of Jacob didn't recognise Joseph the first time, so it was they didn't recognise Jesus the first time He came. But when He comes a second time Zechariah 12:10 says, 'They will look on me, the one they have pierced, and they will mourn.'

When Joseph's brothers came a second time, Joseph revealed himself to them. When they realised it was him they were fearful, but he said to them, 'Don't be afraid . . . You intended to harm me, but God intended it for good to accomplish what is now being done, the saving of many lives' (Genesis 50:19-20).

When Peter addressed the crowd at the beginning of Acts, they realised that Jesus, whom they crucified, was the Messiah. They were cut to the heart, but Peter told them, 'Fellow Israelites . . . I know you acted in ignorance . . . But this is how God fulfilled what He had foretold through the prophets, that the Messiah would suffer . . . Repent and be baptised . . . in the name of Jesus Christ for the forgiveness of your sins.' Three thousand were saved that day and many more since.
(Abbreviated from Acts 2)

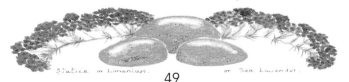

Statice or Limonium.   or Sea Lavender.

Scabious.

When reading this story it struck me how grieved Joseph was because his brothers hadn't recognised him. Seven times he wept. It made me think how it must grieve the heart of Jesus when we or His fellow Jews don't recognise Him as the Messiah.

When Jesus went to Jerusalem, knowing He was facing death, 'He wept over it' (Luke 19:41). He tells His disciples that the chief priests and teachers of the law would condemn Him to death. They would hand Him over to the Gentiles, who would mock Him, spit on Him, flog Him and kill Him (Mark 10:32-34).

So the Gentiles, too, played a part in His death, even though for two thousand years the Jews have suffered much because of it. But like Joseph, Jesus is not resentful. He just longs that they will turn to Him. In Ephesians 2 it says, 'We have been brought near by the blood of Christ . . . [He] destroyed . . . the dividing wall of hostility . . . His purpose was to create in himself one new humanity out of the two' (Ephesians 2:13-15): Jew and Gentile one in Him.

His-story is still on going.

Joseph's storehouse is still open but now Jesus is in charge. He wants to forgive us, feed us and restore us. Philippians 2:10-11 says that one day

At His name every knee shall bow.

Yellow Scabious.   Corn Cockle.

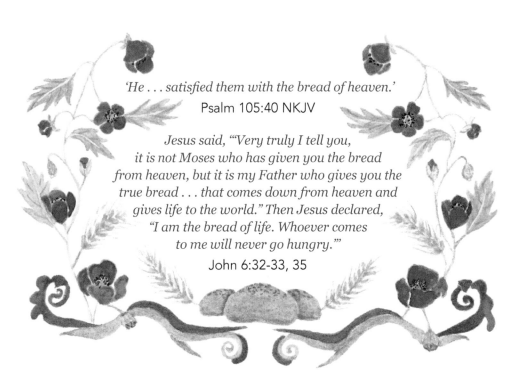

'He . . . satisfied them with the bread of heaven.'
Psalm 105:40 NKJV

Jesus said, "'Very truly I tell you,
it is not Moses who has given you the bread
from heaven, but it is my Father who gives you the
true bread . . . that comes down from heaven and
gives life to the world." Then Jesus declared,
"I am the bread of life. Whoever comes
to me will never go hungry."'
John 6:32-33, 35

The Olive Tree

Olive tree   in   the   Garden   of   Gethsemane.

The olive trees are very long-lived, many claim the oldest trees are approximately eight hundred years old. The indigenous or wild olive tree first appeared in the eastern Mediterranean area, and was then cultivated.

Olive trees featured all through scripture. When Noah sent out a dove to see if the flood had receded, the dove returned with an olive leaf in its beak (Genesis 8:11). Olive oil was used for light in the Tabernacle and spices were added to the oil for anointing (Exodus 25:6, 30:31-33). When the Israelites came back to their land after captivity in Babylon, they celebrated the feast of the Tabernacles and Nehemiah 8:15 says they picked branches 'from olives and wild olive'. The theme of olives extends through to Revelation 11 when it likens the two witnesses that stand before the Lord as the two olive trees.

So how did my quest to find out more about the olive tree start? At a craft fair I found a beautiful card called, PASSION FROM DAY ONE, by a local Christian artist, Liz Cosh. It tells of God's love for us and depicts a baby curled up in the pupil of an eye. It made me want to find where and in what context the 'apple of His eye' is found.

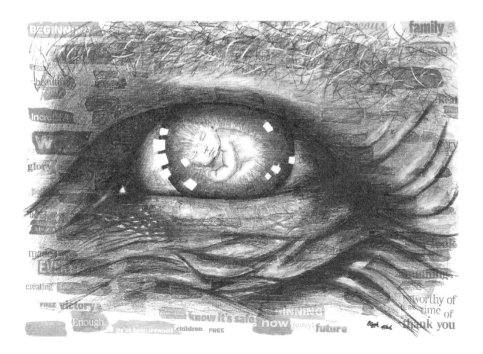

1st Arrangement: The Apple of His Eye

'In a desert land he found him, in a barren and howling waste.
He shielded him and cared for him;
he guarded him as the apple of his eye.'
Deuteronomy 32:10

Eye-shaped arrangements made with willow branches, tied on ends
and dried, phormium leaves for eye brows, gypsophila or hemlock
flowers for the white of the eyes. Roses and apples for eyes.

The first scripture I found is in Deuteronomy. Moses was coming to the end of his life. He had taken the children of Israel out of bondage in Egypt and had lead them for forty years in the wilderness. God told him that Joshua was to succeed him. The Lord also gave him the words to a song that he was to recite and teach to the whole assembly of Israel. Deuteronomy 32:9-12 says,

> 'For the LORD's portion is his people, Jacob his allotted inheritance.
> In a desert land he found him, in a barren and howling waste.
> He shielded him and cared for him;
> he guarded him as the apple of his eye,
> like an eagle that stirs up its nest and hovers over its young,
> that spreads its wings to catch them and carries them on its pinions.
> The LORD alone led him; no foreign god was with him.'

Moses' song was remembered through the ages by the people of God. Years later it was quoted in Psalm 17. David prays that the Lord would 'keep me as the apple of your eye; and hide me in the shadow of your wings'. Also, Zechariah 2:8-9 gives a prophecy against all nations that have plundered or oppressed Israel: 'For whoever touches you touches the apple of his eye – I will surely raise my hand against them.'

From the time of Abraham he and his descendants served the one true God, YAHWEH, who became known as the God of Abraham, Isaac and Jacob (Acts 7:32). God provided, cared, nurtured and fed them, physically and spiritually. He helped them grow in the knowledge and love of Him. David, in Psalm 52:8, says, 'I am like an olive tree flourishing in the house of God; I trust in God's unfailing love for ever and ever.'

Hosea 14:6 says Israel 'will be like an olive tree'.

2nd Arrangement: **The Olive Tree**

'If some of the branches have been broken off,
and you, though a wild olive shoot,
have been grafted in among the others
and now share in the nourishing
sap from the olive root.'
Romans 11:17

Two sections of one piece of wood with arrangement placed on top,
representing Jew and Gentile brought together as one.

So when Paul wrote a letter to the newly planted church in Rome, he likened Israel to a cultivated olive tree. Because of the Roman occupation, the Roman church is believed to be made up of both Jew and Gentile believers. So to iron out any possible friction between the two groups, chapters 9 to 11 are about the cultural differences between them and how they are part of the same root.

Paul wrote that some of the branches of the cultivated tree (the Jews) had been broken off because of unbelief, and to the Gentiles he wrote that they are branches from a wild olive tree, that have been grafted in. He warns them about being proud and boastful; he reminds them that Isaiah prophesied that a stone would be placed in Zion to make Israel stumble. That the Gentiles shouldn't presume to be better than the Jews because they had been grafted in, because it is the root that supports them both and we could all fall into the trap of unbelief, but if we stay connected to this olive tree we share in the nourishing sap from the olive root.

'If the root is holy, so are the branches.'
Romans 11:16

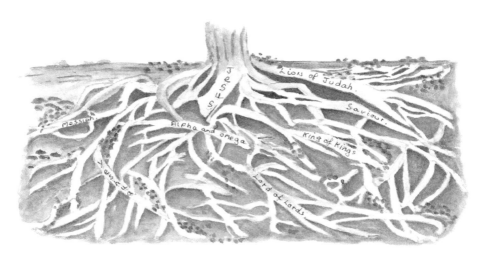

So Paul likens the church to an olive tree with Jew and Gentile as branches, but what of its root? What does he mean when he says, 'If the root is Holy'?

Jesus said, 'I am the Root and the Offspring of David.'
Revelation 22:16

The roots of our faith lie deep in the heart of the God of Abraham, Isaac and Jacob. Roots have to be there at the beginning to allow the plant to grow. Jesus has been there since the beginning. He is at the heart of the temple worship, the feasts and the prophecies that God, in His love, has revealed to us through the prophets. He sent His Son to die in our place. In that wonderful passage in Isaiah 53 that speaks of the crucifixion, it says in verse two: 'He grew up before him, like a tender shoot, and like a root out of dry ground.' The root anchors the plant, feeds it by taking minerals, sugars and water up through the stem, leaves and into the flowers in the form of sap, to give the life-maintaining fluids and food that it needs. Isaiah 49:15-16 says,

'I will not forget you! See, I have engraved you in the palms of my hands.'

Jesus came into the world that was parched and dry, lacking in life-giving nutrients. He came as that Holy Root so that when we are in Him we can receive those life-maintaining fluids and food that we need.

3rd Arrangement: Inscribed in the Palms of His Hands

'I will not forget you. See, I have inscribed you in the palms of My hands.'
Isaiah 49:15-16 NKJV

Arrangement indicating us in the palm of His hands under the cross.

There are many symbolisms in the Bible and the olive tree is no exception.

Firstly: when the olives are ready to be harvested, some are handpicked but most are beaten from the tree with poles or by shaking and they are collected in nets on the ground. The olives are then scourged and crushed to extract the oil.

Jesus was beaten, shaken, knocked to the ground, scourged and crushed, before the oil of the Holy Spirit was released into the lives of believers (John 16:7, 13-15).

Secondly: the disciples saw Him taken up to heaven on the Mount of Olives (Acts 1:1-12). And it is there He will return (Zechariah 14:4).

Thirdly: in Solomon's temple the entrance to the inner sanctuary, where the priests went to pray on behalf of the people on the Day of Atonement, was made from olive wood (1 Kings 6:31-33).

Fourthly: the Garden of Gethsemane lies at the foot of the Mount of Olives, which in Hebrew means 'the garden of the oil press'. In that beautiful olive grove with many ancient trees is the place Jesus took His disciples on the night He was betrayed. It became His 'inner sanctuary' as He prayed to the Father about what was going to take place, that final Atonement!

His soul was overwhelmed and crushed.

Paeonia   Seed head.

Many things took place that day on the cross. Jesus had said at the start of His ministry that He had not come to abolish the Law or the prophets but to fulfil them (Matthew 5:17). 'His purpose was to create in himself one new humanity out of the two, thus making peace . . . to reconcile both of them to God through the cross' (Ephesians 2:15-16).

What the prophets had said was being fulfilled: the requirements of the Law, i.e. the burnt offering, the meal offering, the peace offering as well as offerings for sin, were all fulfilled once and for all. Paul tells us in the letter to the Ephesians 2:11-22 that once, as Gentiles, we were far from the promises of God, but now under the new covenant we are included and grafted in and are joint heirs. He has reconciled us both through His atoning blood. All that is required now is that we believe, repent and receive Him into our lives. That we stay firmly rooted in Him, and that life-giving sap from the Holy Spirit will feed and nourish us, as children of the living God.

Agapanthus

In the first scripture reference it says, 'In a desert land he found him, in a barren and howling waste.' In my study Bible (Strong's Lexicon # 8414: *tohu*) refers to a howling waste, a trackless wilderness, a scene of utter disarray, desolation and barrenness, i.e. sheer emptiness as opposed to order and balance.

Before we come to know Jesus as Lord and Saviour, life can sometimes feel like a trackless wilderness, not having a purpose or sense of direction. Sometimes the world can seem in disarray and desolation.

But He is the Good Shephard who longs to gather His lambs in His arms and carry them close to His heart (Isaiah 40:11). If you have received Him into your lives, then you are 'the apple of His eye'. He will bring order and balance into your life. The nails that pierced the palms of His hands also engraved your name there. We can say with David,

> *'I am like an olive tree flourishing in the house of God;*
> *I trust in God's unfailing love for ever and ever.'*

Psalm 52:8

Praise His Name.

Ipomoea.
'Star of Yelta'.

'Again I ask: did they stumble so as to fall beyond recovery? Not at all! Rather, because of their transgressions, salvation has come to the Gentiles.'

Romans 11:11

'I do not want you to be ignorant of this mystery, brothers and sisters, so that you may not be conceited: Israel has experienced a hardening in part until the full number of the Gentiles has come in, and in this way all Israel will be saved. As it is written: "The deliverer will come from Zion . . . And this is my covenant with them when I take away their sins."'

Romans 11:25-27

The Last Supper

Bulbous Irises.

Popavers.

The Last Supper, as we call it, was the last time Jesus celebrated the Feast of the Passover with His disciples (Matthew 26:17-30).

The ministry of Jesus had started about three years previously. His cousin, John, had been called by God to prepare the way. One day when John was calling the people to repent and be baptised, he was telling them that One was to come who is mightier than him and He would baptise them with the Holy Spirit. When Jesus Himself came along He identified Himself with this message of repentance by asking John to baptise Him. After which He was lead into the wilderness to be tempted by the devil; after forty days and forty nights He was victorious over all temptations. Then the devil left Him and angels came to minister to Him. From there He went to live in Capernaum in the region of Galilee, where He heard that John had been put in prison. Matthew 4:17 says, 'From that time on Jesus began to preach, "Repent, for the kingdom of heaven has come near."'

He called His first disciples to follow Him. As well as preaching and teaching, He feeds the hungry, He heals the sick in mind and body, restores sight to the blind and hearing to the deaf, raises the dead. He explains previously unknown things about the kingdom of God, sometimes using parables.

He predicts His own death (Matthew 17:22-23). When they were staying in Galilee, He said to them, 'The Son of Man is going to be delivered into the hands of men. They will kill him, and on the third day he will be raised to life'. . . but now it was time to make their way to Jerusalem to celebrate 'The Feast of Passover'.

In the apostle John's account of their last meal together, in chapters 13-16 he focuses on their discourse, and the final lessons Jesus wanted His disciples to take hold of.

First: the importance of being 'In Him, feeding on His word and staying attached to the vine.'

Second: humility and selfless service, a love for one another and for the people they serve.

Third: the Holy Spirit will help us with our understanding of the Word and our spiritual growth.

So let us look at what happened at that momentous Last Supper.

Jesus replied, 'The hour has come for the Son of Man to be glorified.'
John 12:23

'On the night he was betrayed, [he] took bread, and when he had
given thanks, he broke it and said, "This is my body, which is for you;
do this in remembrance of me ... For whenever you eat this bread
and drink this cup, you proclaim the Lord's death until he comes.'
1 Corinthians 11:23-26

Jesus knew it was time for Him to return to the Father and that prophecies spoken of Him by David in the psalms were about to be realised. He predicted that a close friend, someone He trusted, one who shared His bread, would betray Him (Psalm 41:9). He also knew a cruel death awaited Him (Psalm 22; Isaiah 53). Yet He was willing to do the will of His Father who sent Him.

During the Passover meal He took the bread, gave thanks and broke it, and gave it to them saying, 'This is my body given for you; do this in remembrance of me.' Then He took the cup saying, 'This cup is the new covenant in my blood, which is poured out for you' (Luke 22:19-20).

The disciples did not understand what was happening. Why was He saying that the bread was His body and the wine was His blood, when it was supposed to represent the slain lamb? At that very first Passover meal, He gently explained to them that He must be lifted up (crucified), that just as Moses had lifted up the serpent in the wilderness to bring life and healing to a disobedient nation, so must the Son of Man be lifted up so that all who believe in Him can have life and healing (John 12:27-50).

So what is the new covenant?

Jesus offers us unconditional love. Just like a marriage between two people, that love calls for a response from both parties. God gave His Son to die for the sin of the world. His body, like the bread, was broken for us, and just as when we receive the bread and eat it, it becomes part of us, when we receive Jesus into our lives and feed on His word, in the same way He becomes part of our life. He is our life-giving bread; He is our sustenance.

The shedding of His blood is the eternal sacrifice for sin, through which we are justified or, as I have sometimes heard it explained:

'Just as if I have never sinned.'

When we bring our sins before Him in repentance we are acquitted. Through the continuing work of the Holy Spirit and the word of God in us, we are also sanctified (John 17:17).

After the meal He explains to them that He is returning to the Father and although at the moment they cannot come with Him, He was going to prepare a place for them and one day He would return to take them with Him to His Father's house. This new covenant would embrace Gentiles too, all those who receive Him into their lives, so we also are heirs to the promises of God, and we too can enter into that Most Holy Place.

2nd Arrangement: Jesus Washes His Disciples Feet

'He poured water into a basin and began to wash his disciples' feet,
drying them with the towel that was wrapped round him.'
John 13:5

'I have set you an example that you should do as I have done for you.
Very truly I tell you, no servant is greater than his master,
nor is the messenger greater than the one who sent him.'
John 13:15-16

Even though Jesus had come from the very presence of God, He had a servant heart. After the meal He removed His outer garments, wrapped a towel round His waist and washed His disciples' feet.

Jesus was sending them out into the world to continue the work He had started. He gave them a new commandment to love one another as He had loved them. Earlier in His ministry He had told His followers, and that includes us, that we are to love our enemies and to pray for those who persecute us. We are to be perfect, just as our Father in heaven is perfect.

Jesus had put others before Himself even to the point of death. He had come to do the Father's will and show love and compassion to a hurting world. He wanted to show the disciples that they too needed a 'servant' heart, so He took on the role of a servant and washed the disciples' feet. They needed to understand that although people would find release and healing through their ministry, it was God who would do the healing. Pride should have no place in their hearts; they were just taking on the role of a servant, just as Jesus had before them (John 13:2-17).

He stressed again the importance of remaining in Him. He explains to them that just as a branch is cut off from the main stem it will wither and eventually die, so they and we must remain in Him. He and His words should become part of our very being, part of who we are. He promises to send a helper, the Holy Spirit, who will strengthen us, teach us and bring to our remembrance all that He has taught us.

Anemone 'de Caen'.

The disciples began talking amongst themselves. They were finding this all too hard to understand:

What does He mean when He says we must remain in Him?
How can we remain in Him when He talks of going away?
What does He mean when He promises to send the Holy Spirit?

> *'What does he mean by saying, "In a little while you will see me no more, and then after a little while you will see me," and "Because I am going to the Father"? They kept asking, "What does He mean by 'a little while'? We don't understand what He is saying."'*

John 16:17-18

What does all this mean?

3rd Arrangement: **He Has Overcome the World**

'Now the prince of this world will be driven out.'
John 12:31

*'Having disarmed the powers and authorities, he made a
public spectacle of them, triumphing over them by the cross.'*
Colossians 2:14-15

Flowers arranged over world shape. World is made by marking out
land shapes on a dried oasis sphere; glue seed (e.g. fennel) on sea
area and spray blue. Wash and dry melon seeds and dye using red
or orange food colouring. When dry glue them on land area,
with cotton wool for North and South Pole.

Jesus saw they wanted to ask Him about this, so He said to them, 'I came from the Father and entered the world; now I am leaving the world and going back to the Father' (John 16:28). He tells them that they will grieve, but they will see Him again and their grief will turn to joy, a joy that no one will take from them. He warns them that they will face problems and persecution, but they must be of good cheer because

'He has overcome the world.'

Rose and Rosemary.

When God created humans, He created them to be in communion with Him. Fruits and plants would be their food; they would have dominion over every living creature. The only thing they were told not to do was to eat from the Tree of Life – which they did. They were banished from the presence of God, they lost that close relationship they had with the Lord their God. Cherubim and flaming swords blocked their way back.

Three things had gone wrong:

First: the world – they disobeyed their creator God in favour of listening to and acting upon other influences.

Second: the flesh – they wanted self-rule, i.e. independence from God.

Third: the devil – they listened to the serpent (devil) when he said this was possible.

When Adam and Eve chose to listen to those influences other than their God, they opened the way for them and the rest of the human race to be in bondage to seen or unseen evil forces – 'principalities and powers', as they are often referred to in scripture. Paul in Colossians 2:8-10, 20 calls it 'the elemental spiritual forces of this world'. 1 John 5:19 says 'that the whole world is under the control [or influence] of the evil one'.

When Jesus came to earth to show us the way back to the Father, He was the only one able to pay the price of sin. He was and is the sinless Son of the living God, in whom all the fullness of God dwells. When He was nailed to that cross along with our sin, He disarmed the principalities and powers, He made a public spectacle of them triumphing over them by the cross (Colossians 2:15). Through His death and resurrection, when we are in Him, when we are attached to the true vine (John 1:1-8) we too can overcome

The World, the Flesh and the Devil.

Iris sibirica.

Summary

John's account of the Last Supper in chapters 13-17 is one of my favourite parts of scripture. When I am really worried about something and I am finding it hard to sleep, I get up, make a cup of tea and turn to these reassuring words.

'Do not let your hearts be troubled.
You believe in God; believe also in me.'
John 14:1

'The Holy Spirit, whom the Father will send in my name,
will teach you all things and will remind you
of everything I have said to you.
Peace I leave with you; my peace I give you.
I do not give to you as the world gives.
Do not let your hearts be troubled and do not be afraid.'
John 14:26-27

In a way it is easier for us to understand than it was for the disciples. They had a preconceived idea that when the Messiah or Anointed One came He would free them from their enemies and reign forever. So they were shocked and confused when He was telling them He had to die. They hadn't realised that the real battle they faced was not with the Romans, but in the heavenly realms. It didn't become clear to them until they saw the risen Lord and received the gift of the Holy Spirit. It can be a bit like that for us too – not really realising who this Jesus is until we accept Him into our lives, allow His blood to cleanse us from all sin, and receive the Holy Spirit. We, too, can then know that inner peace that the world cannot give.

People try all sorts of things to find that inner peace that we all need. Like Adam and Eve we can still seek 'self rule', we can still be taken in by 'deceptive philosophy' and by 'principalities' of this world, some even try occult practices in search of meaning and guidance for their lives (Colossians 2:8-15, 20) but these are the wrong paths to take. We can be like the Gentiles who went to the temple and said to Phillip, 'Sir, we would like to see Jesus' (John 12:21). We too can see and know Him. All we need to do is accept what Jesus has done for us on the cross, receive that 'bread of life' and that life cleansing 'blood' and ask Him for the gift of the Holy Spirit. He will remind us that Jesus said,

'In me you may have peace. In this world you will have trouble.
But take heart!
I have overcome the world.'
John 16:33

'Lord, help us to continually feed on your word, stay attached
to the vine, serve one another with love and humility,
and always remember the freedom we have
through the precious blood of our
Lord Jesus Christ.'
Amen.

'When Christ came as high priest of the good things
that are now already here, he went through the
greater and more perfect tabernacle that is not made
with human hands, that is to say, is not part of this
creation. He did not enter by means of the blood of
goats and calves; but he entered the Most Holy Place
once for all by his own blood, so obtaining eternal
redemption . . . For this reason Christ is the mediator
of a new covenant . . . Christ was sacrificed once to
take away the sins of many; and he will appear a
second time, not to bear sin, but to bring salvation
to those who are waiting for him.

Hebrews 9:11-12, 15, 28

The Emmaus Road

Daphne burkwoodii.   Double Narcissi: Muscari.

One day Cleopas and his friend were walking the seven miles from Jerusalem to Emmaus. They were feeling a bit confused and dejected. They knew that God had promised their ancestor Abraham that they would become a great nation but over the years that hope had been dashed time and time again. The children of Israel had continued to live in Egypt after the time of the famine. God had used Joseph to feed the nations, but after his death a new king had come to power. He forced them into harsh labour and set task masters over them. So for four hundred years they lead a life of bondage until God sent Moses to secure their freedom. Then under the leadership of Joshua they established their homeland in the land of Canaan.

They were governed by prophets and priests until they wanted to be like other nations and have their own king. Under David and Solomon they prospered; after that things deteriorated. There followed a national split when the ten tribes in the north continued to call themselves Israel and the two southern tribes, Judah and Benjamin, became known as the tribe of Judah or the Jews (1 Kings chapters 11 to 12).

Seven hundred and fifty years ago the northern tribes (i.e. Israel) were captured and forced into exile by the Assyrians. Then about one hundred and forty years later the tribes of Judah also were taken, this time by the Babylonians. After seventy years the Jews were allowed to return and the work to restore their temple began (Ezra and Nehemiah). That was four hundred years ago, but here they were again oppressed and ruled by another nation, this time the Roman Empire.

When would it all end?

Pieris japonica 'Variegata.'

1st Arrangement: **The Emmaus Road**

'That same day two of them were going to a village called Emmaus ...
They were talking to each other about everything that had happened.
As they talked ...Jesus himself came up and walked along with them.'
Luke 24:13-15

To include two men with arrangement in the middle to
indicate Jesus joining them as they walked and talked.

Cleopas and his companion had grown up believing that an Anointed One would be sent by God to deliver them from their enemies, and under Him the kingdom would be established. He would be their prophet, priest and king; their Messiah.

They had been following a man called Jesus for the past three years, and had seen Him heal the sick and raise the dead. His inspired preaching drew the crowds. He came into Jerusalem for the Passover festival earlier in the week. It seemed the whole city came out to rejoice and praise God for all the works they had seen. They sang, 'Blessed is he who comes in the name of the LORD' (Psalm 118:26). That psalm speaks of the coming Messiah! Hope was beginning to rise up in them, but a few days before, Jesus had been wrongly accused and crucified. Their hopes were dashed again. Then three days later, when some of the women had gone to the tomb they found it empty. They claimed they had seen a vision of angels who told them He was alive.

What was going on?

As they were thinking over these things Jesus Himself joined them, although they didn't realise it was Him. He started explaining to them all the scriptures concerning Himself, starting with Moses and all the prophets.

Did He remind them that God had told Moses that one day He would rise up another prophet anointed by God, who would lead His people into freedom and a better life?

Did He explain to them that Micah had prophesied the Messiah would be born in Bethlehem (Micah 5:2)?

Isaiah, when he talks of the coming Messiah, says, 'The Lord himself will give you a sign: the virgin will conceive and give birth to a son, and will call him Immanuel' (Isaiah 7:14), which means 'God is with us'.

When Jesus started His ministry on earth, He went into the temple and quoted from Isaiah 61:1.

'The Spirt of the Lord is on me, because he has anointed me to proclaim good news to the poor. He has sent me to proclaim freedom for the prisoners and recovery of sight for the blind, to set the oppressed free.'

Then to those listening He said, 'Today this scripture is fulfilled.' Luke 4:18, 21

They had wondered: who is this man? Could He be the promised

Messiah?

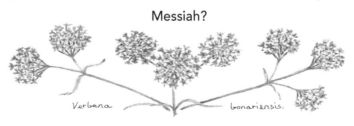

Verbena   bonariensis.

2nd Arrangement: The Prophets

'He said to them, "How foolish you are, and how slow to believe all that the prophets have spoken!" Did not the Messiah have to suffer these things and then enter his glory?" And beginning with Moses and all the Prophets, he explained to them what was said in all the Scriptures concerning himself.'

Luke 24:25-27

To include wooden trumpet shapes in the arrangements, to indicate the prophets' proclamation.

There are many Messianic prophecies in the Old Testament. They speak of His pre-existence with the Father, His birth, who He is, His death, resurrection and His return.

His pre-existence with the Father i.e. the Word: Genesis 1:3; John 1:1-4.
He is the Son of God: Isaiah 7:14; Isaiah 9:6-7.
King of kings and Lord of lords: Psalm 2; Isaiah 32:1-4; Isaiah 33:22.
Our heavenly High Priest: Psalm 110; Zechariah 6:12-13.
Our promised redeemer: Job 19:25-27.
Our good Shepherd: Psalm 23.
Our Judge: Micah 4.
His death: Psalm 41:9; Psalm 22.
His resurrection: Psalm 16:8-11; Psalm 49:15.
His return: Zechariah 14; Joel 2:28-32; Joel 3.

The gift of prophecy is not only about foretelling the future but also interpreting the will of God and pointing people who have wandered from the right path back into a living walk with their maker and sustainer, the Living God.

Hosea was chosen by God to 'live out' the message God wanted to get across to His people. Hosea was to marry a woman who had the spirit of harlotry. The harlotry portrayed in this account shows us that it is one that causes us to be unfaithful to our God, to cease from obeying Him and worship idols instead. When we accept Jesus as our Lord and Saviour we become 'His bride'. Hosea teaches us that we should not be led astray by this spirit of harlotry, but stay faithful to our God.

Elijah is one of the greatest prophets in the Old Testament and also appears in the New Testament when he, along with Moses, met with Jesus on the Mount of Transfiguration (Luke 9:28-36). Under God's anointing he controlled the weather, the widow's flour never ran out, nor did her oil run dry. He restored life to the widow's son (1 Kings 17:1-24). 1 Kings 18 tells us how he gained victory over the prophets of Baal on Mount Carmel, when they both offered a burnt sacrifice without lighting the fire. There was no response from Baal when he was called upon by his prophets, but when Elijah called upon the Lord God of Abraham, Isaac and Israel, He responded with fire: 'The fire of the LORD fell and burned up the sacrifice' (v38).

Elijah had to flee because King Ahab and Jezebel wanted to kill him. Chapter 19:1-9 tells us he was ministered to by angels. When his earthly ministry came to an end he was taken up to heaven while Elisha watched (2 Kings 2:1-18).

Sounds familiar doesn't it?

Although it seems he didn't speak prophetically about Jesus, his life and ministry were a reflection of the coming Messiah, who also controlled the weather, fed the hungry, healed the sick and raised the dead. He gained control over all the powers of darkness at the cross, and His disciples saw Him ascend into heaven.

3rd Arrangement: **The Lamb that was Slain**

'I saw a Lamb, looking as if it had been slain, standing at the centre of the throne, encircled by the four living creatures and the elders.'
Revelation 5:6

'In a loud voice they were saying: "Worthy is the Lamb, who was slain, to receive power and wealth and wisdom and strength and honour and glory and praise!"'
Revelation 5:12

To include a cross draped in wool, to indicate the Lamb on the cross.

Jesus had talked to His disciples about His death many times. When a woman poured expensive perfume on His head, He said it was in preparation for His burial (Matthew 26:6-13), that He would die in Jerusalem (Luke 13:33).

Three times He told them He would be crucified, but He would rise again on the third day (Matthew 16:21; 17:22-23; Luke 18:31-33). Verse 34 says, 'The disciples did not understand any of this. Its meaning was hidden from them, and they did not know what he was talking about.'

Isaiah, in chapter 52:13 through to 53:12, gives a detailed account of the death of Jesus. He was despised and rejected by men, but he took the punishment we deserve, our sin was placed on Him at the cross. He died in our place: 'He was led like a lamb to the slaughter' (Isaiah 53:7). When John the Baptist saw Jesus coming towards him he said,

'Look, the Lamb of God, who takes away the sin of the world!'

John 1:29

As they walked along the road to Emmaus, He gently explains to Cleopas and his friend that these things had to happen that the prophecies about Him had to be fulfilled. As they neared the village the day was nearly over, so they invited Him to dine with them. As He took the bread, gave thanks, broke it and passed it to them, their eyes were opened and they recognised Him but He disappeared from their sight.

They were so excited they headed straight back to Jerusalem to find the disciples, to tell them all that had happened. While they were talking Jesus appeared in the midst of them. They were startled and frightened at first thinking He was a ghost, but He said to them, 'It is I myself! Touch me and see; a ghost does not have flesh and bones.' He showed them the nail marks in His hands and feet. He said to them, 'This is what I told you when I was still with you: everything must be fulfilled that is written about me in the Law of Moses, the Prophets and the Psalms.' He told them, 'The Messiah will suffer and rise from the dead on the third day, and repentance for the forgiveness of sins will be preached in his name to all nations, beginning in Jerusalem' (Luke 24:36-47). Then He took them out of the city to the Mount of Olives. As He was blessing them He was taken up into heaven.

They Worshipped Him

'Then I heard every creature in heaven and on earth and under the earth . . . saying, "To him who sits on the throne and to the Lamb be praise and honour and glory and power, for ever and ever!" The four living creatures said, 'Amen,' and the elders fell down and worshipped.'

Revelation 5:13-14

Paeonia 'Bowl of Beauty'.

Summary

As Christians we often think we are New Testament people, so our interest in the Old Testament is limited. We tend to think that it doesn't apply to us anymore. Looking up the prophecies in the Old Testament concerning Jesus made me realise just how much there is written about Him before He even came to earth to live amongst us.

Sometimes when I watch the news, I think are these 2,600-year-old prophecies coming true? For instance, as already stated, there had been a national split in the tribes of Israel before they were taken into exile by the Assyrians and the Babylonians. We know that the Jews were allowed to return. If this hadn't happened the birth of Jesus could not have taken place in the land of Judah, as the prophets foretold. After His earthly ministry had come to an end they were once again scattered to the four corners of the earth (Isaiah 11:11-12). They were a nation no more! But Ezekiel 37:1-14 prophesied that one day 'these dry bones would live again'. Not only that but verses 15-28 tell us the split in the tribes of Israel would be healed and they would become one nation again and God would bring them back to their own land.

I found another interesting verse in Genesis 49 when Jacob was blessing his sons before his death. Coming to Judah he says, 'The sceptre shall not depart from Judah . . . until Shiloh comes' (Genesis 49:10 NKJV). I looked it up and found there is a place called Shiloh, it's where Joshua set up the Tabernacle when they reached their promised land (Joshua 18:1). It's believed the Ark of the Covenant (the very presence of God) remained there for over one hundred years, until it was captured by the Philistines (1 Samuel 4). It's also the place where Hannah prayed for a son (1 Samuel 1 – 2).

But what does 'until Shiloh comes' mean? My study Bible says the word Shiloh is understood to mean, 'To whom dominion belongs,' or 'He whose right it is to reign' (Ezekiel 21:27).

So when Jacob talks about Shiloh coming is he foretelling the second coming of our Lord? When He will reign and have full dominion. Isaiah 65:17-25 tells us there will be a new heaven and a new earth. Daniel says, 'His dominion is an everlasting dominion . . . that will never be destroyed' (Daniel 7:13-14 and 2:44-45; also Micah 4:1-8). How can we not believe these prophecies when so many concerning Jesus have been fulfilled already, with such accuracy?

When I was thinking how I could sum up this study, one of our elders was speaking at the Sunday service. He was talking about jigsaws and how we need to see the whole picture before we can start piecing it together. I realised that is exactly what we have to do: we have to look at the whole picture concerning Jesus that God has given us in both the Old and New Testaments before we can piece it together to make that glorious picture of His coming Kingdom, that we can be part of through our precious

'Lamb of God'.

*'He was taken up before their very
eyes, and a cloud hid him from their sight.
They were looking intently up onto the sky as
he was going, when suddenly two men dressed
in white stood beside them. "Men of Galilee,"
they said, "why do you stand here looking into the sky?
This same Jesus, who has been taken from you into
heaven, will come back in the same way
you have seen him go into heaven."'*

Acts 1:9-11

Feasts of the Lord
Spring Feasts

Anemone Blada. Narcissus 'Jetfire'. Eranthis ~ Winter Aconite.

When we think of feast days, we associate it with Christmas, when we meet with family and friends to give thanks and celebrate the birth of our Lord Jesus. But the seven feasts given to Moses were instituted by God Himself! 'And the Lord spoke to Moses, saying, "Speak to the children of Israel, and say to them: 'The feasts of the Lord, which you shall proclaim to be holy convocations, these are My feasts'"' (Leviticus 23:1-2 NKJV).

In Hebrew these seven feasts are called His '*Moedim*', which translates to His 'appointed times' (Numbers 9:2). Just as the plan for our redemption was written into the priestly ministry in the Tabernacle, on studying the feasts they too show a pattern.

They are in three groups.

1. The Spring Feasts: Passover, Unleavened Bread and Firstfruits.

2. Then seven weeks later comes the Feast of Weeks.

3. The Autumn Feasts: Feast of Trumpets, Day of Atonement and Feast of Tabernacles.

Each one of God's 'Appointed Feasts' points us to His redeeming plan.

The children of Israel had been in slavery and bondage in Egypt for over four hundred years. 'God heard their groaning and he remembered his covenant with Abraham, with Isaac and with Jacob' (Exodus 2:24), that He would bring them out into the promised land of the Canaanites (Exodus 3:17). So He appeared to Moses in a burning bush, identifying Himself as 'I am' – 'I am' is used many times in scripture to show the many attributes of our God, for instance, as Creator, Saviour, Comforter and in this case Deliverer. After much persuading, Moses, with the help of his brother Aaron, did as God had asked.

The battle for freedom wasn't won with army against army, but in the heavenly realms with the God of Israel showing His power and the Egyptian cultic, magicians and sorcerers, trying to counteract the power of God. By the seventh plague, Pharaoh starts begging for relief and tries to bargain, but then his heart is hardened, and so it went on until the tenth and final plague hits Egypt. The story is in Exodus chapters 7 to 12.

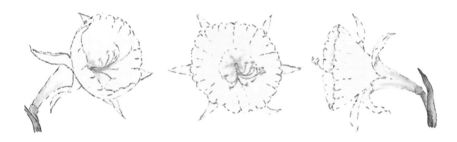

The first and the second of the Spring Feasts, 'Passover' and 'Unleavened Bread', were instituted at this time while they were still in bondage in Egypt. The third Feast called 'Firstfruits' was given to Moses on their way to the promised land. So let us look at these three feasts and see how we too can come into that promised land He has prepared for us in

'His Appointed Time'

1st Arrangement: **'Passover'**

'Then they are to take some of the blood and put it on
the sides and tops of the door-frames of the houses.'
Exodus 12:7

Incorporating a door with arrangements on top
and sides in red flowers to illustrate the blood.

God had already shown Egypt that He was the controller of the natural forces and now He would prove to them that He was also the one who had power over life and death. He would move over the land of Egypt and the firstborn of men and animals would die. 2 Peter 3:9 tells us that our Lord God is patient with us, not wanting anyone to perish.

So He sent Moses to Pharaoh to warn him of the final plague, but still he would not listen, nor let the people go. So God gave these instructions to the community of Israel (Exodus 12).

a) This month shall be a new beginning, it will be called Nisan. God was telling them this is a start of a new future, that they would be a people at one with Him. They would no longer be in bondage, they would be free to worship and serve Him in the land He had promised them (Exodus 6:1-8; also chapter 12).

b) On the tenth day of this month, they were to take a lamb for each household.

c) The lamb will be male without defect.

d) They were to look after the lamb until the fourteenth day, then at twilight it must be slaughtered.

e) No bones should be broken.

f) Take some of the blood and place it on the door posts and on the lintels of their houses.

g) Then they must eat the flesh roasted over the fire with bitter herbs and bread made without yeast.

h) None was to be left till morning, it must all be burned.

i) Eat it with a belt round your waste, sandals on your feet and your staff in your hand.

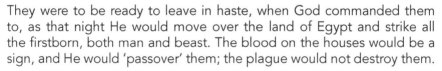

They were to be ready to leave in haste, when God commanded them to, as that night He would move over the land of Egypt and strike all the firstborn, both man and beast. The blood on the houses would be a sign, and He would 'passover' them; the plague would not destroy them.

'When I see the blood, I will pass over you.
No destructive plague will touch you.'
Exodus 12:13

2nd Arrangement: **Unleavened Bread**

'Seven days you shall eat unleavened bread.
On the first day you shall remove leaven from your houses.'
Exodus 12:15 NKJV

Incorporating unleavened bread, representing three Matzahs, one broken. Also first cup of Blessing or Promise, second cup of Deliverance or Salvation, third cup of Redemption and fourth cup of Acceptance.

They were to be ready to leave in a hurry, they couldn't wait for the yeast to rise so no leavened bread could be eaten. In fact they were to eat only unleavened bread for seven days. No leaven (yeast) should be found among them or in their houses. Anyone found with leaven would be cut off from their community (Exodus 13:6-7). To make sure this part of scripture is observed, the night before Passover begins they would search their houses; if any leaven is found, even the smallest crumb, it would be collected and burnt. This second of the spring feasts is so closely associated with Passover that today the festivals are often combined. We are blessed in our church to have a Jewish man and his family. At Easter our pastor asked if he would go through the Passover ceremony with us. We had to wash our hands twice, using a jug of water, a bowl and a towel in a ceremony of cleansing. Then the Matzah or unleavened bread was broken up and we had to take a piece and dip it into a mixture of apple and horse radish, then eat it along with a sprig of parsley (bitter herb). 'They are to eat the meat . . . along with bitter herbs, and bread made without yeast' (Exodus 12:8). The bitter herb was a reminder of the bitterness that being in bondage and slavery can bring.

A cup of wine would be taken as a 'blessing' or 'promise' to bring them out of bondage. Another interesting part of the ceremony that has become a practice over the years concerning the Matzah or unleavened bread, three pieces are wrapped in a cloth, the master of the household takes out the middle piece, breaks it in half and hides one piece for the children to find. (The middle one of the Godhead was broken and placed in a tomb before being 'found' again.)

Then the second cup of wine is taken and speaks of deliverance and salvation. Psalms 113 to 118 are sung at Passover. 'I will lift up the cup of my salvation and call on the name of the LORD' (Psalm 116:13). The story of their deliverance from slavery into the promised land is told. The children then find the bread, which is then broken up and given to be dipped, as explained above.

The third cup of wine speaks of redemption. Just as Boaz took care of his bride Ruth, our kinsman redeemer will take His people as His bride to care for them. This is the cup Jesus takes in Luke 22:20 before going to His death. 'After the supper he took the cup, saying, "This cup is the new covenant in my blood, which is poured out for you."'

After Jesus drank the cup representing the new covenant He said,

'I tell you, I will not drink from this fruit of the vine from now on until that day when I drink it new with you in my Father's kingdom.'
Matthew 26:29

The fourth cup is of acceptance: acceptance of Jesus as the Messiah.

'I ... am the LORD and apart from me there is no saviour.'
Isaiah 43:11

3rd Arrangement: **Firstfruits**

'I bring the firstfruits of the soil that you, LORD, have given me.'
Place the basket before the LORD your God and bow down before him.'
Deuteronomy 26:10

Incorporating a basket containing barley, fruit and honey.

'The priest shall take the basket from your hands and
set it down in front of the altar of the LORD your God.'
Deuteronomy 26:4

Passover and the Feast of Unleavened Bread were instigated while they were in Egypt. The third of the Spring Feasts, the Feast of Firstfruits, was given to Moses while they were on their way to the promised land.

'And the Lord spoke to Moses, saying, "Speak to the children of Israel, and say to them: 'When you come into the land which I give to you, and reap its harvest, then you shall bring a sheaf of the firstfruits.'"'

Leviticus 23:9-10

The sheaf of barley would be given to the priest, who would wave it before the Lord as a wave offering. A lamb without defect would also be offered along with a grain offering of barley ground into flour and mixed with oil and salt, put into a basket along with all the produce of the land, the first of the grapes, figs, pomegranates, honey and wine. The produce would be given to the priest along with praise and thanksgiving to the Lord for His provision in bringing them out of Egypt into this promised plentiful land (Deuteronomy 26:10).

'Firstfruits' was kept through the ages, but there were some kings of Israel who had turned again to pagan worship and they didn't honour the Lord in keeping the feasts. In 2 Chronicles chapters 30 to 31 we see that Hezekiah restores Passover, Unleavened Bread and Firstfruits. Also, after captivity in Babylon, on their return they kept the feasts. The practice of dedicating the firstfruits also included animals and humans (Exodus 13:1-2). Even the first fleece was given to the Lord (Deuteronomy 18:4).

We read in Luke 2:22-23 that when Jesus was born, He too was presented to the Lord. While He was growing up He kept the feasts until His death on the cross thirty-three years later, but as Psalm 16:10 says, 'Because you will not abandon me to the realm of the dead, nor will you let your faithful one see decay.' Death could not hold Him as three days later He rose from the dead.

'But Christ has indeed been raised from the dead, the firstfruits of those who have fallen asleep.'

1 Corinthians 15:20

Viburnum bodnantense.

Liriope muscari. and Spathiphyllum or Peace Lily.

Summary

God told Moses in Deuteronomy 16 that three times a year all the males, including their families, should appear before the Lord their God in the place of His choice, for the Festival of the Spring Feasts, the Festival of Weeks and the Festival of the Tabernacles. During the time of Moses God's chosen place of worship was the Tabernacle, and this continued until the Temple was built in Jerusalem by King Solomon (2 Chronicles 7:1-8:16), which is where Jesus also kept the feasts. All the gospels give the account of Jesus coming into Jerusalem for that final Passover meal, where He likened the 'Passover Lamb' to Himself – see the Passover page: (a) to (i).

1st   (a) In Him we have a new start.

2nd (b) to (e) Tells us the Lamb would live amongst them for a while. He would be without defect (or sin). He would be slaughtered at twilight but no bones would be broken.

3rd   (f) Shows us the blood of the Lamb, Jesus, protects us from all the forces of darkness, but we need to apply it to our lives.

4th   (g) The bitter herbs are a reminder of how living out of the will of God can cause bondage and sin. The bread without yeast is also a reminder that we need to repent of all sin. As with the Feast of Unleavened Bread.

5th   (h) No yeast or leaven must be found on their person, as they travel the path to freedom. We, too, cannot go into God's promised land with unconfessed sin. So just as when we partake of the 'bread and wine' in our Communion services, we too must examine ourselves and be right before God and also with one another. Our commitment to Him must be total because His precious sinless body was broken for us, and His blood when applied to our lives will protect and cleanse us from within to set us free.

One last thought . . .

6th   (i) Reminds me of Ephesians 6 on the 'Armour of God'. We, too, must go on to the promised land with the belt of truth, sandals of readiness to talk about our God and be equipped with the sword or staff – the Word of God.

'Firstfruits' (1 Corinthians 15) speaks much of the resurrection. It tells us that Christ died for our sins, was buried but rose again on the third day according to scripture, that because He rose from the dead, He became the 'Firstfruits' of those that are in Christ at His coming. When our earthly corruptible body will be raised incorruptible, for in Adam we all die, but if we are in Christ at His coming we too will be raised, just as He was, incorruptible. James 1:18 says,

'He chose to give us birth through the word of truth,
that we might be a kind of firstfruits,
of all he created.'
Praise His Name

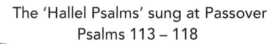

Scilla.

The 'Hallel Psalms' sung at Passover
Psalms 113 – 118

Psalm 118
'Give thanks to the Lord, for he is good;
his love endures for ever. Let Israel say:
"His love endures for ever." Let the house
of Aaron say: "His love endures for ever."
Let those who fear the Lord say:
"His love endures for ever."'
v1-4

'The Lord is with me; I will not be afraid.'
v6

'The Lord is my strength and my defence;
he has become my salvation.'
v14

'You are my God, and I will praise you;
you are my God, and I will exalt you.
Give thanks to the Lord, for he is good;
his love endures for ever.'
v28-29

The
Wilderness Years

The Wild Bunch.

Many of the Old Testament prophets, Isaiah, Jeremiah, Daniel, etc., went through wilderness experiences, sometimes persecuted for their faith or with their own doubts and fears. David, too, went into the wilderness in En Gedi in the area of the Dead Sea when King Saul was pursuing him (1 Samuel 24:1-2). Also, his psalms are full of his doubts and fears that we too can identify with.

The conversion of Saul of Tarsus, later known as the apostle Paul, was sudden and dramatic after only a few days of darkness and confusion. He went on to serve the Lord and wrote the Epistles in the form of letters to the early church that we still learn from today. We don't all experience conversions like that; for most of us it's a step-by-step learning process, sometimes making mistakes, but growing closer to our Lord day by day. That's why I like to read John Bunyan's *The Pilgrim's Progress*. After coming through the 'gate', which is Christ, Christian journeys through life, learning as he goes, until he comes to the Celestial City. We learn how Christian coped when he found himself in a wilderness of doubt and despair.

It's a bit like the Exodus story. The children of Israel were released from a life of bondage by the shed blood of the Passover lamb. Under the leadership of Moses they were set free to find the land God had promised them many years before. At that time the Egyptians worshipped many gods; they had a sun god, a moon god and even a crocodile god, but now the children of Israel would be free to worship the one God, the God of their fathers, Abraham, Isaac and Jacob (Exodus 9:1). Because they had been living in a pagan culture for about fourteen generations, they had much to learn. The story is found in Exodus, Leviticus, Numbers and Deuteronomy.

The gospels also tell us of a time at the start of the ministry of Jesus. He, too, was led by the Spirit into the wilderness. So let us look at these examples and find a way that will help us when we go through our wilderness experience.

'Now these things occurred as examples to keep us from setting our hearts on evil things.'
1 Corinthians 10:6

Dandelion and Bird's-eye.

1st Arrangement: The Wilderness

'The LORD your God has blessed you in all the work of your hands.
He has watched over your journey through this vast wilderness.
These forty years the LORD your God has been with you,
and you have not lacked anything.'
Deuteronomy 2:7

Representing a path through the wilderness.

'Your ears shall hear a word behind you, saying,
"This is the way, walk in it."'
Isaiah 30:21 NKJV

God wants us to be free from any kind of bondage, whether it is to do with our past, circumstantial, preconceived ideas or just wrong attitudes. So let us take a brief look at what God teaches us through the time the children of Israel spent in the wilderness.

Sometimes when we are making a new start and following a different path in life, one of the hardest things to do is to let go of the past. So God, not wanting them to change their minds and turn and go back to Egypt, took them by the way of the wilderness. When they reached the Red Sea they realised that the Egyptians were pursuing them. Their past was catching up with them. They were terrified. Immediately their minds were filled with doubts and fears. What have you done bringing us out of Egypt? Are we going to die in the desert? Maybe it would have been better for us to continue to serve the Egyptians! But Moses answered the people: 'Do not be afraid. Stand still, and see the salvation of the LORD . . . The LORD will fight for you, and you shall hold your peace' (Exodus 14:13-14 NKJV). That's exactly what did happen; the Lord saved His people once again.

'The Israelites saw the mighty hand of the LORD displayed against the Egyptians . . . and put their trust in him and in Moses his servant.'

Exodus 14:31

However, their new-found faith didn't last for long. When they reached the Desert of Sinai and made camp, Moses went up the mountain to seek guidance from the Lord. Because he was gone a long time, the people, with the help of Aaron, made a golden calf. When Moses came down from the mountain he was angry with them for making their own god to worship and sacrifice to (Exodus 32). Their lack of faith and grumbling continued. They craved the good food that they had in Egypt, so God gave them quail and manna. They complained that the water was bitter so God made it sweet, then another time He gave them the pure water from the rock (Exodus 16 – 17). When they reached the borders of Canaan, God sent one from each tribe to spy out the land; ten of them came back saying there were giants and no way could they claim the land for themselves, even though God had promised it to them. Only Joshua and Caleb believed that God would lead them and give them the land (Numbers 14:6-9). So because of their unbelief, instead of reaching their promised land in eleven days they wandered round and round in the wilderness for forty years.

By then none of those that had refused to believe that God had said this land was to be theirs were left alive – they had died in the wilderness. Only Joshua and Caleb, who had believed God, were allowed to enter into the promised land.

Cotton (iris)

'Some sat in darkness, in utter darkness, prisoners suffering in iron chains . . . They stumbled, and there was no one to help. Then they cried to the LORD in their trouble, and he saved them from their distress. He brought them out of darkness . . . and broke away their chains. Let them give thanks to the LORD for his unfailing love.'

Psalm 107:10-15

'Do not gloat over me . . . Though I have fallen, I will rise. Though I sit in darkness, the LORD will be my light.'

Micah 7:8

John Bunyan, in his book *The Pilgrim's Progress*, uses picture language to explain the different situations and people that Christian meets on his way to the Celestial City.

One day he and Hopeful were following a path and next to them was a river called the River of the Water of Life. Growing on the banks of the river were trees with all different kinds of fruit, so they ate, drank and rested by this river. Then the path and the river seemed to go in different directions and the path got very rough; the stones were beginning to hurt their feet. Eventually they came to a style and saw that the path on the other side was easier going, convinced that this path was also going in the right direction, so they took it. They soon realised they were lost, as the path they had taken led them into the grounds of Doubting Castle, the owner was Giant Despair. He captured them and took them to his castle, and put them in a very dark dungeon. He left them there for many days and nights, with no food, drink or friends. They tried to encourage one another, but their situation grew worse. Giant Despair battered them constantly with thoughts and feelings, filling their minds with doubts, fears, depression and anxiety. Their problems started to get the better of them; they began to feel discouraged, lonely, worried, unworthy – literally crushed in spirit.

Do you sometimes suffer under those thoughts from the giant despair?

How did Hopeful and Christian find release from this giant? One really dark night they began to pray. Then in the early hours of the morning Christian realised something and said to Hopeful, 'What a fool I am. I forgot that I have the key to get us out of this stinking dungeon. It will open any lock in Doubting Castle.'

It is called **Promise.**

When we hold the word of God and His promises to us, in our hearts and lives, we can unlock any sort of bondage that the Giant Despair wants to pull us down into.

In Romans 8:31-39 Paul tells us:

'If God is for us, who can be against us? . . . Who then is the one who condemns? . . . Who shall separate us from the love of Christ? Shall trouble or hardship or persecution? . . . No, in all these things we are more than conquerors through him who loved us. For I am convinced that neither death nor life, neither angels nor demons, neither the present nor the future, nor any powers . . . in all creation, will be able to separate us from the love of God that is in Christ Jesus our Lord.'

Wild Strawberry.

3rd Arrangement: **Jesus in the Wilderness**

'Then Jesus was led by the Spirit into the wilderness
to be tempted by the devil . . . Jesus answered, "It is written:
'Man shall not live on bread alone, but on every
word that comes from the mouth of God."'
Matthew 4:1-4

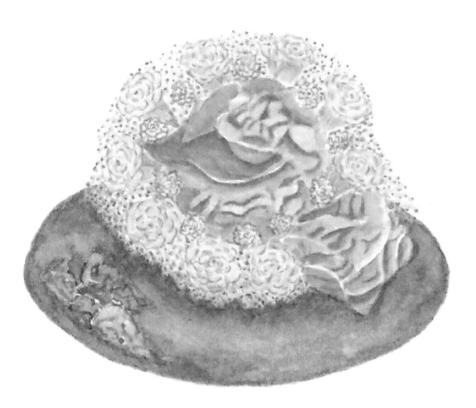

In the centre of the arrangement is a 'Desert Rose' (crystal). This rosette crystal is a formation on minerals, which tend to occur in arid sandy conditions, such as the evaporation of a shallow salt basin.

'The wilderness and the solitary place shall be glad for them;
and the desert shall rejoice, and blossom as the rose.'
Isaiah 35:1 KJV

The Old Testament often points to a time when a Messiah would come. Isaiah prophesied in chapter 40:3 that it would be preceded by a 'voice of one calling: "In the wilderness prepare the way for the LORD."' We understand now this refers to John the Baptist, a cousin of Jesus, who spent most of his early life in the wilderness, until the word of God came to him as to his mission. 'He went into all the country around the Jordan, preaching a baptism of repentance for the forgiveness of sins' (Luke 3:3). One day Jesus came to him to be baptised and we read the Holy Spirit descended on Him. Matthew, Mark and Luke all record this. Scripture also tells us that after His baptism, He was led by the Spirit into the wilderness for forty days to be tempted by the devil (Luke 4:2-13).

a) Jesus was hungry, so the devil said to Him, 'If you are the Son of God, tell this stone to become bread.' Jesus answered, 'It is written: "Man shall not live on bread alone"' (Deuteronomy 8:3).

b) The devil then took Him to a high mountain and said, 'If you worship me, it will all be yours.' Jesus answered, 'It is written: "Worship the Lord your God and serve him only"' (Deuteronomy 6:13).

c) The devil then led Jesus to Jerusalem and had Him stand on the highest point of the temple. Then the devil started to use scripture also, but out of context. 'If you are the Son of God, throw yourself down from here. For it is written: "He will command his angels concerning you to guard you . . . they will lift you up"' (Psalms 91:11-12). Jesus replied once again using the commands that God had given to Moses in the wilderness (Deuteronomy 6:16): 'Do not put the Lord your God to the test.'

Crimson clover.

Sometimes I wonder why Jesus had to experience forty days of wilderness and temptation. After all, He is part of the Godhead: the Son of God, the Word that became flesh. But that makes what He has done for us more amazing. He identified Himself with us in every way.

He was born with human limitations. He knew what it was like to be homeless, He experienced hunger, thirst, physical pain, also the pain of feeling lonely, deserted by His friends, forsaken by His heavenly Father as well as being tempted to step out of the will of God by the devil. He too counteracted the wrong thoughts that could have led to wrong actions, by using the word of God found in the scriptures.

He is our prime example. He took on human form so that through His death He could bring many believers to glory and guide them to that Celestial City.

The wilderness years have so much to teach us about God's love and compassion. Healing and wholeness is not a new thing; it has always been what God wants for us. At the start of **Exodus** God reveals Himself to Moses as the God of their fathers, the 'I Am', the one who is and is to come. The one true God. He delivered them out of bondage, He provided for them with food and water, their clothes never wore out. He gave them the Ten Commandments and instructions for living. He taught them the pattern for worship and gave them the Tabernacle, a place to worship.

In **Leviticus** He calls them into holiness; it is mentioned about eighty times. We are to be holy as He is holy. We are not saved because we are holy but to be holy. We are human and we do sin, but He knows our hearts and our desires to be more like Him. Although even in these writings of Moses, we see the people's lack of faith and grumbling. We find His grace offered to them time and time again. He gave them manna, 'bread from heaven' (Jesus) and the pure water of life (Jesus, 1 Corinthians 10:4).

In **Numbers** we find two censuses listing everyone by name. God wants to know each one of us as individuals. One thing that stops us from entering into that promised land is unbelief. Romans 1:17 says, 'Just as it is written: "The righteous will live by faith."' We see that those who refused to believe that God would take them safely home died in the wilderness. Those that remained, as they reached the point of crossing over the River Jordan into the promised land, were counted again.

Deuteronomy reminds us again what God requires of us, His instructions for living are reinforced. He calls for our obedience, assures us of God's blessings and that He wants us to enter into a covenant relationship with Him. Before his death Moses gives the people a prophetic message of the coming Messiah. He recites a song to the people reminding them of all that God had done for them, and the covenant He made with them. Then Moses gave them his final blessing, and Joshua takes over and takes them to the promised land.

When I read the story of Jesus in the wilderness I see that each time He replied to the temptations from the devil, He used the instructions given to Moses in Deuteronomy. We must use the word of God to counteract the thoughts planted in our minds by the enemy of our souls, just as

Christian used the promises of God when he found himself in the depths of despair. He could say with David,

*'I waited patiently for the L*ORD*; he turned to me and heard my cry. He lifted me ... out of the mud and mire; he set my feet on a rock and gave me a firm place to stand. He put a new song in my mouth, a hymn of praise to our God.'*

Psalm 40:1-3

'Let all the people say, "Amen!"'

Psalm 406:48

The Priestly Blessing

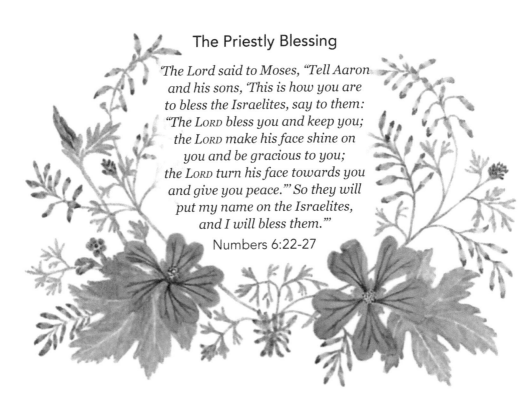

*'The Lord said to Moses, "Tell Aaron and his sons, 'This is how you are to bless the Israelites, say to them: "The L*ORD *bless you and keep you; the L*ORD *make his face shine on you and be gracious to you; the L*ORD *turn his face towards you and give you peace.'" So they will put my name on the Israelites, and I will bless them.'"*

Numbers 6:22-27

Feast of Weeks

Or

Shavuot

Chinese Tree Peonie

We look again at the seven feasts God gave to Moses, that were to be His holy convocations or His *Moedim*, which translates to 'His appointed times' (Leviticus 23:1-2). If you remember, the first two feasts, Passover and Unleavened Bread, remind us that Jesus our Saviour is the sinless Lamb of God who died so we may be free from the power of sin and its final consequence, death. The third feast, Firstfruits, points to how He conquered death and if we truly belong to Him we too will live. Jesus said,

'I am the resurrection and the life.
He who believes in Me, though he may die, he shall live.'
John 11:25 NKJV

The feasts seem to follow the pattern of the harvest. The Firstfruits was when they brought the first of the barley to the Lord. Seven weeks later the barley crop comes to an end and the final harvest of wheat begins, starting with the Feast of Weeks and ending in the autumn with the Feast of Tabernacles, which is the completion of the harvest when all the crops are gathered in.

'You shall observe the Feast of Weeks, of the firstfruits of wheat harvest.'
Exodus 34:22 NKJV

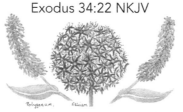

So what part of His *Moedim* or appointed time does this fourth feast point to? Sometimes, as with the Torah and the prophetic messages given to us by the prophets, we don't understand its full meaning until we see it taking place or the Holy Spirit reveals it to us. In Hebrew the word Shavuot means Weeks, hence this convocation is referred to as Shavuot or Feast of Weeks. As Christians we are more familiar with the Greek word for Shavuot, which is Pentecost. We know it as the time when the Holy Spirit came upon the early believers. Filled with the Holy Spirit the message of the gospel spread. As they started to reach out to other lands, the believers called themselves Christians or Christ followers and for many years the coming of the Holy Spirit was celebrated at the same time as our Jewish forefathers, fifty days after the resurrection. It was also classed as a holiday for us called Whitson. But in 1971 the holiday in England was replaced by a fixed date at the end of May and called Spring Bank Holiday, although the day itself is still recognised in our churches.

So let us look at this amazing day in history and what it means for us today.

1st Arrangement: **Ezekiel's Vision**

'As I looked ... I saw a wheel ... they would go
in any one of the four directions.'
Ezekiel 1:15-17

'When the living creations moved, the wheels beside them moved.'
Ezekiel 1:19

'Wherever the spirit would go, they would go,
and the wheels would rise along with them,
because the spirit of the living creatures was in the wheels.
Ezekiel 1:20

Incorporating four wheels, one holding the arrangement.
Wheat for the wave offering and two loaves made with yeast.

They were to count fifty days after the Feast of the Firstfruits (Leviticus 23:15-22). As well as the required animals for sacrifice they were to bring a grain offering. This time it would be wheat as the wheat harvest was just beginning. Some of the grain would be ground into fine flour and made into two loaves, this time made with leaven (yeast). They would be given to the priests as a wave offering and a blessing before the Lord. There would be a drink offering, a burnt offering, a sin and a peace offering. It was to be a holy convocation; no work should be done and no wheat was to be eaten until the first cut had been presented to the Lord at the Temple.

In the early Christian era of 'Anno Domini' the Temple had been destroyed and they could no longer sacrifice. The rabbis made it into a celebration of the giving of the Law and the birth of Judaism. The synagogues were decorated with flowers. The Torah was studied. The book of Ruth was also looked at, as the life of Ruth is very dear to their hearts. She was not a Jew, but had married into a Jewish family. When her father-in-law and her husband died, her mother-in-law, Naomi, wanted to return home to Judah. Ruth decided not to return to her own people but committed herself to Naomi with these well-known words, 'Where you go I will go . . . Your people will be my people and your God my God' (Ruth 1:16). She went on to help in the barley fields of Boaz; eventually they married and she became the great-grandmother of King David. The genealogy follows right through to Jesus, Yeshua, the Messiah.

The Holy Spirit is referred to many times in the writings of Ezekiel. In the first chapter, which is also read, Ezekiel has a vision of God coming in the form of wind and fire, and wheels moving in every direction, symbolising going out into all the world. The final reading takes them to the prayer of Habakkuk, which says in chapter 3:2 (NKJV):

'O LORD, revive Your work in the midst of the years!
In the midst of the years make it known; in wrath remember mercy.'

Sunflower
"Teddy Bear"

2nd Arrangement: Like a Dove

'Jesus also was baptised; and while He prayed, the heaven was opened.
And the Holy Spirit descended in bodily form like a dove upon Him.'
Luke 3:22 NKJV

'When He, the Spirit of truth, has come, He will guide you into all truth.'
John 16:13 NKJV

'Like a dove descending' – I used dried branches of a fishbone
cotoneaster horizontalis sprayed white. White or blue flowers.

Our God 'did revive His work in the midst of the years'.

One day, about six hundred years after Habakkuk penned this prayer, God sent His Son (John 1:1-14). 'The Word became flesh and made his dwelling among us' (v14). He came in the form of a baby, to live on this earth as one of us, for approximately thirty years. He lived and grew as we do. He and His family lived like any other Jewish family, attending His place of worship and keeping the feast days. The Holy Spirit had been with Him all the way; He was conceived by the Holy Spirit. When He was only twelve years old the teachers of the Law were amazed at His understanding of scripture. When He was baptised by John the Spirit of God descended on Him like a dove. He was anointed by the Spirit for ministry (Luke 4:18).

He began to preach and expound the scriptures. He calls twelve disciples, and they saw Him calm the wind and waves, heal the sick, the paralysed and raise the dead. When He cast out unclean spirits, even the demons recognised who He was (Luke 4:31-36).

Allium Siculum.

One day a Pharisee named Nicodemus came to Jesus to ask about His teaching (John 3:1-21). Jesus tells him he must be born again, born of the Spirit, and that if he really understood the scriptures he should know these things, i.e. that the Christ would suffer, rise again, that repentance and remission of sins should be preached, and then the Holy Spirit power would come (Luke 24:44-49).

It is a must, not an option, because the Holy Spirit is our Helper, Comforter and Advocate: He will convict the world of sin, righteousness and judgement. He will teach us all things and remind us of what Jesus had said when we forget (John chapters 14 to 16). He will point us to

Jesus and we will know that He is the only way to God. He will guide us into all truth, and help us to live by it. He builds us up in the faith (Ephesians 1:17-19; Jude 20). He brings peace, joy and hope.

All three persons of the Godhead are mentioned in Ephesians 1. Paul tells us of God's grace in verse 3. In Jesus we have redemption and forgiveness through His blood (v7) and we are sealed with the Holy Spirit guaranteeing our inheritance (v13).

What a wonderful Lord and Saviour we have. But after three short years His time on earth was coming to an end. There was one final trial Jesus had to go through before the Father's plan of redemption could come to pass.

'O Lord ... in wrath remember mercy.'
Habakkuk 3:2 NKJV

John the Baptist said, 'I baptise you with water for repentance.
But after me comes one who is more powerful than I . . .
He will baptise you with the Holy Spirit and fire.'

Matthew 3:11

'But when he, the Spirit of truth, comes, he will guide you into all the
truth. He will not speak on his own; he will speak only what he hears,
and he will tell you what is yet to come.'

John 16:13

Incorporating the elements of wind and fire.

After the darkest day in history, when even the sun refused to shine, God's plan of redemption was beginning to take shape. The promised new covenant would come like 'wind and fire' and spread throughout the world (Ezekiel).

In the midst of the years he begins to make it known. (Habakkuk)

The disciples, Mary, His brothers, along with some other faithful followers, had met in Jerusalem. Together they prayed and wondered what would happen next. They remembered that just seven weeks ago, when Jesus was still with them, they had gone to Jerusalem to celebrate the spring feasts of Unleavened Bread, Passover and Firstfruits. When Jesus had been betrayed and arrested by the authorities, He was mocked, flogged, spat on, then crucified. They had treated Him worse than the sacrificial lamb! Even though He had done nothing wrong. They thought it was all over, but after three days He rose again. Over the next forty days He appeared to them many times. The last time they saw Him, He reminded them what John the Baptist had said: 'He will baptise you with the Holy Spirit and fire.' Then they went with Him to the Mount of Olives where they watched as He ascended back to His heavenly Father. He had told them to wait in the city of Jerusalem until they 'receive power when the Holy Spirit comes on you' (Acts 1:8).

Ten days later, the day came when they would normally be celebrating Shavuot, the promise was fulfilled:

'When the day of Pentecost [Shavuot] came ... Suddenly a sound like the blowing of a violent wind came from heaven ... They saw what seemed to be tongues of fire ... All of them were filled with the Holy Spirit.'

Acts 2:1-4

Peter, who a few weeks before, through fear, had denied his Lord, stood up and addressed the crowd that had gathered. With boldness and Holy Spirit insight he told them what they had just seen taking place had been prophesied by Joel and other prophets. The people were so shocked and fearful they cried out to Peter, 'What shall we do to be saved?' Peter tells them, and us, that we must repent and believe in Jesus Christ for the forgiveness of our sins. To be baptised (fully immersed) in Jesus and the reality of who He is and what He has done for us and we will receive the gift of the Holy Spirit.

Crocosmia

Summary

The Day of Pentecost is a familiar story, but three things have left questions in my mind.

First, why did the instructions for this feast include two loaves made with leaven? We realise now that the unleavened bread used at the Passover feast pointed to our sinless Saviour. Do these two loaves represent the human race, both Jew and Gentile, still with sin (leaven) in our lives, being presented to the Lord God at the beginning of the final harvest? Jesus often speaks of the harvest and likens it to His harvest of people. One day He said to His disciples, 'The harvest is plentiful but the workers are few. Ask the Lord of the harvest, therefore, to send out more workers into his harvest field' (Matthew 9:37-38).

Second, why wind? We cannot see the wind only feel its effects. Strong winds can bring destruction, as in Job, or a storm at sea as Jonah experienced. But in scripture we see when we have problems the wind of the Spirit of God is with us. When Noah had been on the ark for one hundred and fifty days, God sent a wind and the waters subsided (Genesis 8:1). In the wilderness a wind was sent out by the Lord and brought back food (Numbers 11:31). When we read of Paul's journeys round the Mediterranean Sea, it was governed by the wind (Acts 27). When we have times of trouble and anxiety we can be tossed about by the storm, but, when God sends the wind of His Holy Spirit into our lives, He comes in power but also as a gentle breeze. He comes to restore, bring peace, to teach, feed us spiritually and guide us.

Third, why fire? We have all seen on the news the damage Australian bush fires can do. The firefighters sometimes bring them under control by lighting another fire round the perimeter, so that when the bush fires reach the burnt area they go out as there is nothing left to burn. The late preacher Selwyn Hughes once said, 'There are two fires burning in this world. There is the fire that ravages and the fire that redeems.'

When God called Moses, it was from the midst of a bush that appeared to be on fire, but it did not burn up (Exodus 3). The fire that came from God changed him from living in fear, to a life of faith. After his early insecurities needing the help of his brother, he became one of the all-time greats. His faith had been refined by the fire of God, which made him more precious than gold (1 Peter 1:7).

'He will be like a refiner's fire . . . and refine them like gold.'
Malachi 3:2-3

In Matthew 3:12 John continues saying,

> 'His [Jesus] winnowing fork is in his hand . . . gathering his wheat
> [His final harvest] into the barn and burning up the chaff.'

He, by His Holy Spirit, is like the 'refiner's fire' which burnt out the impurities in our lives, so we too can be used as workers in His harvest field.

God wants us to be in a personal and right relationship with Him. His plan of redemption includes us receiving His Holy Spirit as with His very first followers on the Day of Pentecost. So if you are saying: how can I receive the Holy Spirit? I would say to you, if you have accepted Jesus as your Lord and Saviour, and your heart longs for more of Him, read Luke 11:9-13. Ask, knock and seek. One word of warning: only seek the Holy Spirit through the shed blood of our Lord Jesus Christ, because there are counterfeits. 1 Timothy 2:5 says, 'There is one God and one mediator between God and mankind, the man Christ Jesus.'

Jesus said in Luke 11:13

> 'If you then, though you are evil, know how to give good
> gifts to your children, how much more will your Father in
> heaven give the Holy Spirit to those who ask him!'

So keep asking, knocking and seeking until you receive
that wonderful anointing on your life.
Then like a fire when it burns it reaches up to the
heavens, so your whole being, mind, body and spirit
will reach up like tongues of fire to worship Him
(John 4:21-24).

John 4 v, 21-24

131

The Armour of God

Anemone, Dahlia,   Echinacea & Begonia

When I became a Christian, the minister who led me to the Lord, wrote down for me Ephesians 6:14-18 on the armour of God, together with a brief explanation as to the meaning. He told me that along with my prayer time I should put on the armour of God daily. I understand it was something he and his wife did each morning, along with praying for guidance from the Holy Spirit as to who he should visit or speak to that day. He brought more people, both inside the church and out, into a living relationship with our Saviour than anyone I have ever known.

So before looking at Paul's letter to the Ephesians, let us take a brief look at the background. A few years ago we visited the site of the ancient port town of Ephesus. We were amazed at how well preserved it was. We walked down the marble streets with tall columns and statues on either side. There were homes, a shop area with mosaic flooring, baths and latrines. At the end of the main street was a very impressive building, believed to be the library, where twelve thousand parchments were found during excavation. Down another street we came to a market place; it was not far from the port where ships would come in, bringing traders who would sell their wares at the market. A few miles out to sea is the Isle of Patmos, where John wrote the book of Revelation while being held as a prisoner for preaching the gospel.

There was also a large amphitheatre, which could hold up to twenty-five thousand people. This is where the Bible tells us in Acts 19:23-40, that a riot broke out against Paul and the Christians that were with him when the people felt their goddess Artemis, later known as Diana, was being discredited. In fact the Temple of Diana in Ephesus was one of the seven wonders of the ancient world. Only one column remains on the site. Instead stands a basilica to Saint John. Tradition says that John settled in Ephesus and it is believed that Mary the mother of Jesus also lived there as Jesus had entrusted her care into John's hands.

So let us look at what Paul says to the Ephesian church and to us about putting on the whole armour of God.

Amphitheatre
Ephesus.

1st Arrangement: **Paul Prays**

'That the God of our Lord Jesus Christ, the Father of glory,
may give you . . . wisdom and revelation in the knowledge of Him . . .
that you may know . . . the hope of His calling . . .
[and] the riches of the glory of His inheritance.'
Ephesians 1:17-18 NKJV

'I pray that out of his glorious riches he may strengthen
you with power through his Spirit in your inner being,
so that Christ may dwell in your hearts through faith.'
Ephesians 3:16-17

In Paul's letter to the Ephesians, he begins by stressing the need to know their walk and where they stand in Christ. To know His power to reign, His majesty, His authority, His strength, His dominion, His might (Jude 24-25). They really had to understand more of the God they had decided to serve. He prays for them, mentioning all three persons of the Godhead.

'That the God of our Lord Jesus Christ, the Father of glory, may give to you the spirit of wisdom and revelation in the knowledge of Him.'

Ephesians 1:17 NKJV

We need to remember this Gentile church, before coming to faith in Christ Jesus, had been at the centre of the worship of the pagan goddess Diana. So Paul feels the need to remind them, that once they walked according to the world and the principality and power of the air, but now by the grace of God they have found redemption and forgiveness of sins, through the blood of Jesus and they were sealed by the Holy Spirit. That they are now joint heirs with Israel, fellow citizens with God's people, members of the household of God, built on the foundations of the prophets and apostles with Christ Jesus as the chief cornerstone. They were members of one body, Jew and Gentile, and, as such, they share in the promises of God.

Paul prays again, for the whole family of God:

That we walk in love, as Christ loved us.
That we walk in unity, as there is one body, one Spirit,
one Lord, one God the Father.
That we walk in the light, as He has brought us out of darkness into the light.
That we walk in wisdom, so we do not give the devil a foothold.

Paul tells the Ephesians and the Corinthians that to stand against the devil's schemes, they need to put on the whole armour of God and stand by the word of His truth, by the power of God and by the armour of righteousness. Recognising that the spiritual battle often goes on in our minds, so they and we must learn to meditate and memorise scripture, so we can take captive every thought that is hostile to God and make it obedient to Christ.

Ephesians 6:10-13; 2 Corinthians 10:1-5

2nd Arrangement: The Belt, Breastplate and Shoes

'Stand firm then, with the belt of truth . . .
the breastplate of righteousness . . .
and with your feet fitted with the readiness
that comes from the gospel of peace.'
Ephesians 6:14-15

'And I pray that you, being rooted and established in love,
may have power . . . to grasp how wide and long and high
and deep is the love of Christ, and to know this love . . . that
you may be filled to the measure of all the fullness of God.'
Ephesians 3:17-19

Having made sure they know their walk, where they stand
in Christ and prayed they will know the fullness of God,
Paul says to the Ephesians in chapter 6:10-11

'Finally, be strong in the Lord and in his mighty power. Put on the full armour of God, so that you can take your stand against the devil's schemes.'

First, 'Stand firm then, with the belt of truth buckled round your waist . . .' (v14).

In the world today many believe there is no absolute truth; that people should live by what feels right for them. But in the end that brings chaos, confusion and lawlessness because, whether we like it or not, God has placed unseen forces in this world to keep it going as He designed, for example gravity, the sun that rules the day, the moon that rules the night and the tides. The whole of nature has been created to have a natural rhythm, including the human race, which He designed in His image, breathed life into and gave instructions to live by. We must be people who not only speak the truth, but live by the truth of the word of God. John 8:31-32 says,

'If you hold to my teaching, you are really my disciples.
Then you will know the truth, and the truth will set you free.'

Second, '. . . with the breastplate of righteousness in place . . .' (v14).

Isaiah prophesied in chapter 59:16-17 that the redeemer would come and bring salvation, and that He would have on the breastplate of righteousness. In this fallen world we cannot make our own righteousness. We have to be 'in Him' and take on ourselves 'His breastplate'. In 1 Peter 1:15-16 it says,

'Just as he who called you is holy, so be holy in all you do;
for it is written:"Be holy, because I am holy."'

Third, verse 15 says,

'And with your feet fitted with readiness that
comes from the gospel of peace.'

We must always be ready to bring this gospel of peace to a hurting world. Luke tells us in chapter 12:35 to be ready for service, and Paul when he writes to the Roman church in chapter 10:14-15 also refers to the well-known verse in Isaiah 52:7,

'How can they believe in the one of whom they have not heard? . . .
And how can anyone preach unless they are sent? As it is written:
"How beautiful are the feet of those who bring good news!"'

'In addition to all this, take up the shield of faith, with which you can extinguish all the flaming arrows of the evil one. Take the helmet of salvation and the sword of the Spirit, which is the word of God.'
Ephesians 6:16-17

'Now to him who is able to do immeasurably more than all we ask or imagine, according to his power that is at work within us, to him be glory.'
Ephesians 3:20-21

Paul continues in verse 16,

> 'In addition to all this, take up the shield of faith, with which you can extinguish all the flaming arrows of the evil one.'

Fourth, 'Take up the shield of faith . . .'

Over the years many voices, or flaming arrows, have come against faith in the one true God. Once I was told the Bible was just papier-mâché and news print! What happened to believing that the Bible is the inspired word of God that lights our path (Psalm 119)? I have heard the virgin birth denied! What happened to believing that the Holy Spirit came upon Mary and she conceived the son of God (Luke 1)? I have heard the resurrection denied! What happened to believing that Jesus said, 'I am the resurrection and the life' (John 11:25)? I have heard people say there are other paths to God! What happened to believing that Jesus said, 'I am the way and the truth and the life. No one comes to the Father except through me' (John 14:6)?

When you hear these extreme views said, whether they come from inside or outside the church, test them by scripture and if found to be untrue, reject them as a destroying flaming arrow.

Fifth, 'Take the helmet of salvation . . .' (v17).

Why take the helmet of salvation? The enemy of our souls will work on our minds as he did with Eve. He started to make her doubt the word of God by saying, 'Did God really say that?' God had told them they would surely die if they ate from the tree of knowledge of good and evil, but the snake told her she would not die. He tried to tell her what God had said was untrue. But because it looked good and would give her independence from God, she and Adam ate; and because of that, mankind lost the close walk they had with their God. The devil is the father of lies that feeds our fears and makes us doubt the word of God. But James tells us that when we submit ourselves to God, and resist the devil, he will flee from us (James 4:7). He continues by saying, 'Come near to God and he will come near to you.' So take on the helmet of salvation, won for us by the blood of Jesus, and find deliverance from sin, liberation and restoration.

'In Him we have life.'

Sixth, '. . . the sword of the Spirit, which is the word of God' (v17).

So let us take hold of the sword of the Spirit, which is the word of God, and speak that word of faith into every situation that confronts us and counteract every thought the enemy plants into our mind.

'For the word of God is alive and active.
Sharper than any double-edged sword,
it penetrates even to dividing soul and spirit,
joints and marrow; it judges the
thoughts and attitudes of the heart.'

Hebrews 4:12

Oats: Phlomis or
Jerusalem Sage

Polemon 'Heaven Scent'
or Jacob's Ladder.

If the enemy of our souls was defeated at the cross, why is the father of lies still causing us problems? We as Christians can claim victory through the blood of Jesus. But God's plan of redemption still has prophecies to be fulfilled. When the disciples asked Jesus what was going to happen, He told them that they (the Jews) would fall by the sword and be taken to all the nations, and Jerusalem would be trampled on by the Gentiles until the times of the Gentiles are fulfilled (Luke 21:24). Paul often testified that he had been told by God that the gospel should be preached to the Gentiles too, until the full number had come in (Romans 11:25). Revelation 12 tells us right from the time Jesus was born the devil (dragon) tried to destroy the work Jesus came to fulfil, but he couldn't. Verse 17 says, 'He was enraged at the woman and went off to wage war against the rest of her offspring – those who keep God's commands and hold fast their testimony about Jesus.'

'For our struggle is not against flesh and blood, but against the rulers, against the authorities, against the powers of this dark world and against the spiritual forces of evil in the heavenly realms.'

Ephesians 6:12

Paul tells the Ephesian elders to 'keep watch over yourselves and all the flock' because he knew that after he left, savage wolves would come amongst them because the evil one is the master of disguise (Acts 20:28-29). When Jesus was speaking to the crowds in the Sermon on the Mount He warns them: 'Watch out for false prophets. They come to you in sheep's clothing, but inwardly they are ferocious wolves' (Matthew 7:15).

They pretend to be followers of the Lord but they are not.

This is not to make us afraid. We are on the most important journey we will ever make. It's like when we are driving a car: we know that accidents can happen, but we don't drive in fear; we drive with care and being aware of the unexpected.

So let us be aware of the enemy of our souls, but not fearful as we have the victory in Christ. When He was on the earth He prayed that we would be protected from the evil one. Now He has returned to the Father and is our High Priest who is constantly before the throne of grace, on our behalf. All the powers of darkness have now been made subject to Him and one day He will return and His and our victory will be complete.

'Praise be to the God and Father of our Lord Jesus Christ,
who has blessed us in the heavenly realms
with every spiritual blessing in Christ.'

Ephesians 1:3

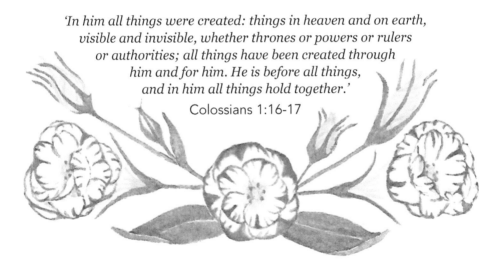

'In him all things were created: things in heaven and on earth,
visible and invisible, whether thrones or powers or rulers
or authorities; all things have been created through
him and for him. He is before all things,
and in him all things hold together.'

Colossians 1:16-17

Law *and* Grace

Amaranthus or
Love-lies-bleeding.

Many years ago I was looking after a man who was terminally ill. One morning while I was there his minister came to give him communion. He asked me to join them. After the minister left we were discussing what it means to be saved, and the subject of Law and grace came up. His thoughts on it are something I have thought about many times since. He said,

> 'Yes we are saved by grace, but because we are saved,
> we want to live according to the Law.'

I thought this was a simple but profound statement. When I was growing up the teaching I received was more on the lines of believe in Jesus as Lord and Saviour and obey the Law. A few years ago the emphasis seemed to change to: we are not saved by obeying the Law, but by grace! OK, sounds good but what about the Law? Do we still obey it or not? I'm sure I am not the only one who has wondered about this. So out comes my concordance to find all the Bible references on Law and grace.

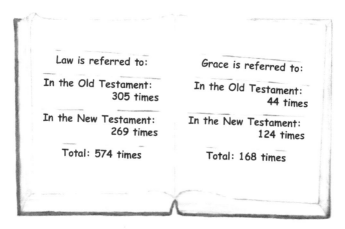

Law is referred to:

In the Old Testament:
305 times

In the New Testament:
269 times

Total: 574 times

Grace is referred to:

In the Old Testament:
44 times

In the New Testament:
124 times

Total: 168 times

God had made mankind in His own image. 1 Peter 1:14-16 tells us that He is holy and wants us to be holy too. But we are inclined to go our own way. So while the children of Israel were in the wilderness, God gave Moses the Law and told him to write it down for future generations. But Paul says in Ephesians 2:5,

> *'It is by grace you have been saved.'*

So let us look at this seemingly 'double-edged sword' and
find the right balance in our walk with the Lord.

'I delight to do Your will, O my God,
and Your Law is within my heart.'
Psalm 40:8 NKJV

*'For I have kept the ways of the L*ORD*;*
I am not guilty of turning from my God.
All his laws are before me;
I have not turned away from his decrees.'
2 Samuel 22:22-23

Moses said,

'They are not just idle words for you – they are your life.'
Deuteronomy 32:47

There are Ten Commandments that we could think of as absolute law, written by God on tablets of stone and kept in the Holy of Holies inside the Ark of the Covenant. But most of them could come under the heading of 'Instructions for Living', as there is advice on what to eat, the best materials to use for clothing, mould in our homes, marriage and moral principles, monitory offerings, as well as how to conduct our worship. For example, the design of the Tabernacle, offerings for sin, trespass and peace, etc. It cautions us against disobedience, and reminds us of the blessings brought by obedience. Numbers 15:22-31 tells us there is a difference between unintentional sin and premeditated sin.

Joshua continued in the same way as Moses, encouraging the people to keep the law and grow in godliness, through knowing and applying God's word to their lives. David also, even though he wasn't perfect, loved the Lord. The psalms are full of 'his delight' in the law and how he loved to meditate on it. Just before he died he instructed his son, Solomon:

'Observe what the LORD your God requires: walk in obedience to him, keep his degrees and commands, his laws and regulations, as written in the Law of Moses.'
1 Kings 2:3

After Solomon, the kings did not encourage the people to honour God, so the people started to disobey their God. Hezekiah tries to bring them back by destroying the places of idol worship, but after his death, his son Manasseh rebuilt them, and the scripture says the Lord was not honoured until Josiah became king. He found the Book of the Law and was grieved when he realised the sins of his fathers. He got rid of mediums and spiritualists and restored the Covenant and the requirements of the Law (2 Kings chapters 22 to 23). But by chapters 24 to 25 we see the return of kings that turned away from God.

Until they were taken into captivity.

After seventy years the tribes of Judah returned. Ezra looked again at the Law and Nehemiah prayed for forgiveness for himself and for the people of Israel. Together they helped to rebuild their city.

The prophets also honoured the word of God and kept the Law, even coming under persecution for it like Daniel being thrown to the lions. Jeremiah also confronted the false teachers of the Law (Jeremiah 14:14) for speaking from their own thoughts and not from the word of God. His heart ached for the people that they should be in the right covenantal relationship with their God. The Lord told them and us that one day He would make a new covenant with His people.

'I will put my law in their minds and write it on their hearts.
I will be their God, and they will be my people.'
Jeremiah 31:33

Pampas grass plumes

Dried, coated in   Wallpaper paste & shaped.

152

2nd Arrangement: **Grace**

*'He has saved us and called us to a holy life – not because of
anything we have done but because of his own purpose and grace.
This grace was given us in Christ Jesus before the beginning of time.'*
2 Timothy 1:9

*'Concerning this salvation, the prophets,
who spoke of the grace that was to come to you,
searched intently . . . trying to find out the time
and circumstances to which the Spirit of Christ in them
was pointing when he predicted the sufferings of the Messiah
and the glories that would follow.'*
1 Peter 1:10-11

In Proverbs 4 Solomon talks of wisdom as listening to and keeping the instructions of the Father and not forsaking the Law. He goes on to say this wisdom will be like a garland to grace your head.

When God the Father gave His Son to the world, He offered to us unmerited favour – 'grace'.

'The Word became flesh and made his dwelling among us ... [He was] full of grace and truth ... Out of his fullness we have all received grace.'
John 1:14, 16

In Acts we see God's grace at work in the apostles (4:33). Stephen was the first believer to die for his faith. It says he was 'full of God's grace and power' (6:8). A man called Saul was a strong believer in the teachings of the Law. He witnessed Stephen's death and approved! That was the day persecution of the church started. Many Christians were driven out of Jerusalem, but they continued preaching wherever they went. Saul was one of the instigators. He began going from house to house putting the believers who remained in prison (Acts 7 to 8) until he was confronted by the risen Lord Jesus (chapter 9). God sent Ananias to pray for him; he was filled with the Holy Spirit. The Lord had both physically and spiritually opened his eyes. His ministry and letters to the churches contain much on the subject of Law and grace and how to rightly apply both to our lives. Saul became known as the apostle Paul.

In Paul's letter to the Romans 6:1 he poses the question: If we are saved by grace, can we, or should we, continue to sin, so grace may abound?' He answers with a definite response: 'Certainly not.' If we have promised the Lord we will die to sin, we cannot live any longer in it. Paul goes on to explain that when we were baptised into Christ Jesus we were baptised into His death, so just as Jesus was raised from the dead, we are raised into newness of life, set free from sin, into His grace.

To the church in Galatia he wrote,

'Walk in the Spirit, and you shall not fulfil the lust of the flesh ... If you are led by the Spirit, you are not under the Law ... But the fruit of the Spirit is love, joy, peace, long suffering, kindness, goodness, faithfulness, gentleness, self-control. Against such there is no law.'
Galatians 5:16-23 NKJV

Garland of fruit.

'Certain individuals . . . have secretly slipped in amongst you.
They are ungodly people, who pervert the grace of our God
into a licence for immorality.'

Jude 4

'You then . . . be strong in the grace that is in Christ Jesus.'

2 Timothy 2:1

3rd Arrangement: Grace Poured Out for Us

'I will pour on the house of David . . . the Spirit of grace . . .
they will look on Me whom they pierced.'
Zechariah 12:10 NKJV

'In him we have redemption through his blood, the forgiveness of sins,
in accordance with the riches of God's grace.'
Ephesians 1:7

What did Jesus say on Law and grace?

Looking through the gospels I realised Jesus had a lot to say on Law. He also had a lot to say to the Pharisees and the teachers of the Law. Their teaching was authoritative and hard. They professed to be righteous but their conduct didn't show it. They put heavy burdens on the people because of their wrong interpretation of the Law (Matthew 23:4; Luke 11:46). The teaching of Jesus often counteracted their interpretation. In 1 Timothy 1:8 it says, 'The law is good if one uses it properly.'

Some teachers of the Law were impressed by His knowledge and wanted to follow Him, but others were constantly trying to trap Him with their questions. When they couldn't they secretly started scheming to have Him arrested and killed. One day they came to Him along with an expert on the Law and asked Him, 'Which is the greatest commandment in the law?' Jesus replied:

> *'"Love the Lord your God with all your heart and with all your soul and with all your mind" . . . And . . . "Love your neighbour as yourself. All the Law and the Prophets hang on these two commandments."'*
> Matthew 22:37-40

Then another time when He was speaking to the people He said:

> *'Do not think that I have come to abolish the Law or the Prophets; I have not come to abolish them but to fulfil them.'*
> Matthew 5:17

What did He mean by saying that He had come to fulfil the Law? From the time of Adam and Eve the death of an innocent animal was used to cover their sin. We are told that God killed and then used an animal skin to cover their shame. This followed on into the sacrificial system at the time of Moses. With sacrifices for sin, trespasses and peace, etc. When Jesus came a new covenant was put in place, even though it reflected the old, as Hebrews 10 tells us. Also, Jesus said what the prophets had prophesied had to be fulfilled. Isaiah 53:7 tells us, 'He was led like a lamb to the slaughter.' He became that sacrificial lamb. He paid the price for our sin and His punishment brought us peace. He is our peace (John 14:27).

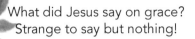

What did Jesus say on grace?
Strange to say but nothing!

But!

Most of the words of grace point to Him. Luke 2:40 says,
'The grace of God was on him.'

John 1:16 says, *'Out of his fullness we have all received grace.'*

He is our grace.

Bougainvillea.

'The mind governed by the flesh is death,
but the mind governed by the Spirit is life and peace.'
Romans 8:6

'So do not fear, for I am with you;
do not be dismayed, for I am your God.
I will strengthen you and help you; I will
uphold you with my righteous right hand.'
Isaiah 41:10

'For all the promises of God in
Him are Yes . . . and . . . Amen.'
2 Corinthians 1:20 NKJV

'The eternal God is your refuge,
and underneath are the
everlasting arms.'
Deuteronomy 33:27

'You shall keep them,
O Lord, You shall preserve
them . . . forever.'
Psalm 12:7

'You are my hiding-place;
you will protect me from trouble.'
Psalm 32:7

'Casting all your care upon Him,
for He cares for you.'
1 Peter 5:7 NKJV

'He will cover you with his feathers,
and under his wings you will find
refuge; his faithfulness will be
your shield.'
Psalm 91:4

'The Spirit of the Lord is upon me,
because He has anointed me to
proclaim good news to the poor.
To set the oppressed free.'
Luke 4v18

'For the Lord delights in you.'
Isaiah 62:4

'"Lo, I am with you always,
even to the end of the age." Amen.'
Matthew 28:20 NKJV

'Beauty for ashes, the oil of joy for mourning,
the garment of praise for the spirit of heaviness.'
Isaiah 61:3

This simple but true story illustrates both law and grace, permit me to share it with you.

Many years ago when our children were small, we were taking them to feed the ducks on our village pond. Although at that time it was quite a small village with not many cars, to get to the pond we had to cross a road. From an early age we had taught them the Highway Code (Law). The two eldest had run on ahead and arrived at the pond safely. Our youngest daughter, so eager to get there with her little bag of duck food in her hand, had just reached the road. In an instant we realised she wasn't going to stop. Her father, noticing a car coming round the bend, just had time to shout to her to stand still. Instantly she froze on the side of the road. He reached her side, took hold of her hand and reminded her to always use the Highway Code. Together they reached the pond safely (Grace). Because she loved and respected her father and knew that he loved her, for him to command her to do something, it must be for her own good, even though it wasn't what she wanted. She obeyed and it may well have saved her life. It reminded me of our heavenly Father. He has given us a 'Highway Code', not to bind or restrict us, but to help us to stay happy, healthy and fulfilled on this journey of life. *That's what we call Law* because He wants us to stay safe and have a happy, fulfilled life.

Scripture tells us *grace* is at the heart of all three persons of the Godhead.

God the Father
'The Lord is compassionate and gracious,
slow to anger, abounding in love.'
Psalm 103:8

'God so loved the world that he gave his one and only Son,
that whoever believes in him shall not perish but have eternal life.'
John 3:16

Jesus the Son
He willingly went to the cross, with our sin placed on Him.
'The one and only Son, who came from the Father,
full of grace and truth.'
John 1:14

'Out of his fullness we have all received grace . . . For the law was given through Moses; grace and truth came through Jesus Christ.'
John 1:16-17

Holy Spirit
'I will pour on the house of David . . . a spirit of grace.'
Zechariah 12:10

Hebrews 10 tells us we can insult the spirit of grace. But when we repent and receive Jesus into our lives we enter into a new covenant with God. Through the sacrifice of Jesus and receive the Holy Spirit, He will write the Laws of God on our hearts and minds.

So when life's problems come our way and our path seems unsure and we don't know the way forward, we can feel hurt, confused and lonely. Listen for the voice of our heavenly Father when He says, 'Be still, and know that I am God' (Psalm 46:10). He will take our hand and gently point us to His Word of life and guide us back to the right path.

That's grace.

So I say to my dear friend, 'Yes, we are saved by faith, by the grace of our wonderful Lord and Saviour, and because we have seen how much He loves us, we love Him too and want to live according to His laws.

'May the grace of our Lord Jesus Christ, and the love of God, and the fellowship of the Holy Spirit be with you all.'
2 Corinthians 13:14

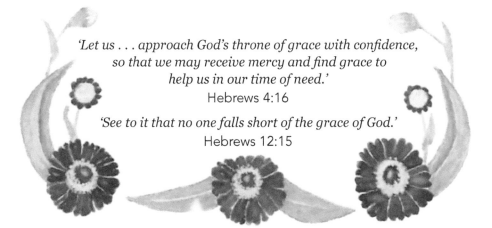

'Let us . . . approach God's throne of grace with confidence, so that we may receive mercy and find grace to help us in our time of need.'
Hebrews 4:16

'See to it that no one falls short of the grace of God.'
Hebrews 12:15

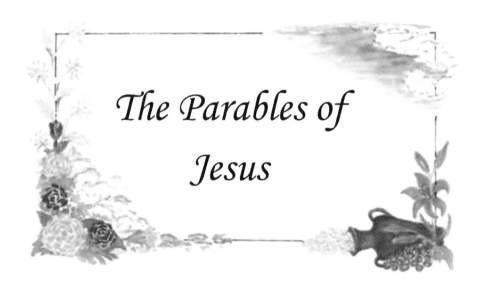

The Parables of Jesus

Zinnia.   Cerinthe minor.

The dictionary definition of the word 'parable' is 'a story used to illustrate a moral or spiritual lesson', or as I have sometimes heard it explained in church, an earthly story with a heavenly meaning.

Jesus often used parables to illustrate certain teachings. Once, after He had been speaking to the people, His disciples came to Him and asked Him why He spoke in parables? He told them that the mysteries of the kingdom of heaven are not made known to everyone and the prophecy of Isaiah was being fulfilled, which says:

> *'Hearing you will hear and shall not understand, and seeing you will see and not perceive; for the hearts of this people have grown dull.'*

He goes on to say:

> *'But blessed are your eyes for they see and your ears for they hear.'*
> Matthew 13:10-16 NKJV

One day a rich young ruler came to Jesus and asked how he could enter the kingdom of God. Jesus knew that in his heart his wealth and position in life meant more to him than his commitment to God. So Jesus told him to sell all he had and give the money to the poor and to come to follow Him. But the man could not do it and went away sorrowful. Jesus turned to His disciples and said,

> *'Again I say to you. It is easier for a camel to go through the eye of a needle than for a rich man to enter the kingdom of God.'*
> Matthew 19:24 NKJV

To be rich and to hold an important position in life is in itself not wrong. It's when riches, status and material things mean more to us than a right relationship with our God. So let us look at some of the parables of Jesus that teach us about the kingdom of God, our attitudes and our part in it.

1st Arrangement: **He is Our Rock**

*Jesus said, 'Whoever comes to Me and hears My sayings and does them
... is like a man building a house, who dug deep and laid the foundation
on the rock ... When the flood arose, the stream beat vehemently against
that house, and could not shake it, for it was founded on the rock.'*

Luke 6:47-48 NKJV

*'The Lord is my rock, my fortress and my deliverer;
my God is my rock, in whom I take refuge.'*

Psalm 18:2

*'Come, let us sing for joy to the Lord;
let us shout aloud to the Rock of our salvation.*

Psalm 95:1

Jesus tells us that the kingdom of heaven is like a mustard seed, that when it is planted in us grows like a tree, and when we are tired and snowed under with problems of this world, in it we can find a place of refuge and rest (Matthew 13:31-32).

In another parable Jesus tells us He is the only way to God. He is the gate to the sheepfold. He is the gate to the kingdom of God. He is the good shepherd who is willing to, and did indeed give His life for us (John 10:7-18).

He warns us the way is narrow and few will find the right path. Most will prefer to go their own way, or worship idols, or think there is no God at all (Matthew 7:13-14). In Luke 12:16-21 we see how we can fall into the trap of the 'bigger barns' syndrome, where Jesus warns about covetousness, always wanting bigger and better things. Verses 22-34 go on to say a happy and fulfilled life doesn't exist of material things that we possess, but we should find our happiness and fulfilment in coming into a living relationship with our God.

Just before Jesus concludes the Sermon on the Mount He says to them, 'Why do you call me, "Lord, Lord," and do not do what I say?' (Luke 6:46).

Then He tells them of two builders. The first builder dug deep and solid foundations on rock, so when the problems came and floods arose and the winds beat against the house it did not fall because it was built on solid rock; meaning we are to build our lives on the solid rock of God and His word. But the builder who hears the word but does not put it into practice, is like one who builds his life on sand. As we all know, when waves come in they move the sand; likewise the wind can blow it around. It is not firm ground. If our life depends on the latest fashion in clothes or new cars or the latest 'in thing' it changes from year to year – but the word of God stands forever.

Paul tells the Corinthians that the lessons learnt by the Israelites in the wilderness still apply to us today. When they wanted to go their own way and put other things (idols) in place of their God . . . but though they didn't realise it Jesus was right there with them. He was the 'Cloud' they followed, He was the 'Bread' from heaven that they received, He was the 'Water from the Rock'.

> *'They all ate the same spiritual food and drank the same spiritual drink; for they drank from the spiritual rock that accompanied them, and that rock was Christ.'*
> 1 Corinthians 10:3-4

He is our Rock.

Place of the Skull   The Rock of Sacrifice   Garden Tomb.

'I am the vine; you are the branches.
If you remain in me and I in you, you will bear much fruit:
apart from me you can do nothing.'
John 15:5

'Jesus answered, "Very truly I tell you, no one can enter the
kingdom of God unless they are born of water and the Spirit."'
John 3:5

'But when he, the Spirit of truth, comes, he will guide you into all the
truth. He will not speak on his own; he will speak only what he hears,
and he will tell you what is yet to come.'
John 16:13

'Seek first the kingdom of God and His righteousness, and all these things shall be added to you. Therefore do not worry about tomorrow.'
Matthew 6:33-34 NKJV

Most of the parables point us to a very important fact,
that we must receive Him into our lives and allow Him
to be in every part of our daily walk with Him.

Just before He went to the cross, Jesus told His disciples that as branches have to be attached to the vine and may need pruning in order to bear fruit, we also may need pruning (John 15:1-8). In other words, there will be things about us we need to change; our worldly attitudes have to be replaced by:

'Not my will, but yours.'

He tells the multitudes who were listening to Him that before they decide to follow Him they must 'count the cost'. He tells them a parable of a man who wants to build a tower: first he will sit down and work out the cost to see if he has enough money to complete it (Luke 14:28-30). Then He goes on to give another example (v31): 'Suppose a king is about to go to war against another king. Won't he first sit down and consider whether he is able with ten thousand men to oppose the one coming against him with twenty thousand?'

He wants us to be a people who will put Him at the centre of our lives, to be salt and light to a hurting world (Matthew 5:13-16), to always forgive those who wrong us or hurt us in any way (Matthew 18:21-35), to be persistent in prayer (Luke 11:1-8), to be a worker in His harvest field (Matthew 9:37-38), bring people to know Him wherever that desire leads us.

To do this we must first do as He says, when He said, 'Repent, for the kingdom of heaven is at hand' (Matthew 4:17 NKJV). To repent doesn't just mean being sorry for your sins; it means to change direction, change our thinking and our purpose in life. If you decide to do this, Jesus warns us not to be left empty (Matthew 12:43-45). Jesus said:

*'No one puts new wine into old wineskins;
or else the new wine bursts the wineskins.'*
Mark 2:22

We need to become a 'new creation', not living according to the ways of the world and following our natural desires. To bring our thoughts, our words and our deeds in line with His will, we need a new spirit within us: we need His 'Holy Spirit'.

169

Even David, Israel's king, when he saw the beauty of Bathsheba, another man's wife, his desire for her led him into adultery and to abuse his position as king. He put her husband in a position of danger, where he would lose his life, so he himself could have her. When he realised he had not only sinned against himself and others but he had sinned also against his God, he cried out to God in repentance, for mercy, saying,

'Create in me a clean heart, O God, and renew a steadfast spirit within me. Do not cast me away from Your presence, and do not take Your Holy Spirit from me.'

Psalm 51:10-11 NKJV

'He answered and said to them, "When it is evening you say,
'It will be fair weather, for the sky is red'; and in the morning,
'It will be foul weather today, for the sky is red . . .' Hypocrites!
You know how to discern the face of the sky, but you cannot
discern the sign of the times."'
Matthew 16:2-3 NKJV

'Let not your heart be troubled; you believe in God, believe also in Me.
In My Father's house are many mansions . . . I go to prepare a place
for you . . . I will come again and receive you to Myself;
that where I am, there you may be also.'
John 14:1-3 NKJV

One day the scribes and Pharisees asked Jesus for a sign; He wouldn't give them one. Instead He told them that just 'as Jonah was three days and three nights it the belly of a great fish, so will the Son of Man be three days and three nights in the heart of the earth' (Matthew 12:40 NKJV). Another time when they were trying to trap Him, He told the parable of the tenants (Matthew 21:33-46).

It was about a land owner (God) who planted a vineyard. He then went away and left it in the charge of the vinedressers (the religious leaders). When he thought the fruit (the people or believers) should be ready to harvest, he sent his servants (the prophets) to collect his fruit, but the vinedressers wanted to keep the fruit for themselves and they treated the servants badly. They were beaten, stoned and some were killed. So last of all, he sent his son (Jesus) but the vinedressers threw him out of the vineyard and killed him too.

Verse 45 says:

'When the chief priests and the Pharisees heard Jesus' parables, they knew he was talking about them. They looked for a way to arrest him.'

Jesus knew He was going to die and who would plot to bring this about, but He also knew that in three days He would rise again, and one day return.

In many parables He points to His return.

'But of that day and hour no one knows,
not even the angels of heaven, but My Father only ...'
Matthew 24:36-44 NKJV

We don't know when that will be, but just as when we look to the sky to interpret the weather, we must also know what the Bible says will be the signs of His return. He wants us to continue to do His will and to use the talents He has given us. He knows that some will give up the wait and go back to their old ways, or fail to keep the light of their faith burning.

He tells the parable of the ten virgins. Five were wise, with enough oil in their lamps to keep their light, or faith, burning. The other five were foolish and allowed their oil to run out. So when the bridegroom (Jesus) came for them, they were not ready (Matthew 25:1-12). Also Luke 12:35-48 tells us of two servants. One had waited patiently for his master's return, the other gave up the wait and began to get drunk and beat the other servants. Jesus said that they would be assigned a place with unbelievers. But ...

'Blessed are those servants whom the master,
when he comes, will find watching.'
Luke 12:37 NKJV

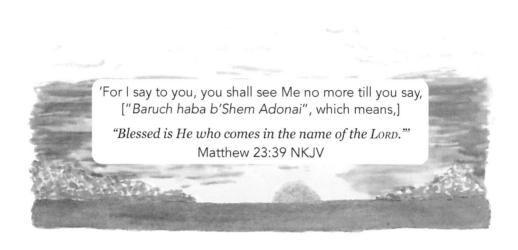

'For I say to you, you shall see Me no more till you say,
["*Baruch haba b'Shem Adonai*", which means,]

"Blessed is He who comes in the name of the Lord."'
Matthew 23:39 NKJV

Arisaema sikokianum

Summary

We can learn so much from the parables. We see Jesus as the way into the kingdom of God. We see the standards of this world aren't necessarily the right way to go. When we decide to follow Jesus our focus in life has to change. The rich young ruler couldn't give up his wealth, and the scribes and the Pharisees could not see even though they used the word of God to gain status. They couldn't or didn't want to see that the word of God points to its fulfilment in Jesus. At the very start of the ministry of Jesus, He says,

> *"'Repent, for the kingdom of heaven is at hand."*
> *... Then He said [calling His disciples], "Follow Me."'*
> Matthew 4:17, 19 NKJV

We not only need to follow Him but also to do what He says and take off the 'old wineskins' and seek the gift of the Holy Spirit to teach us and guide us down the right path.

> *'If you love me, keep my commands. And I will ask the Father,*
> *and he will give you another advocate to help you and be*
> *with you for ever – the Spirit of truth.'*
> John 14:15-17

> *'Seek first the kingdom of God and His righteousness,*
> *and all these things shall be added to you.*
> *Therefore do not worry about tomorrow.'*
> Matthew 6:33-34 NKJV

Winter Jasminum.

One of the parables I had always found a problem with was the one about the workers in the vineyard (Matthew 20:1-16). A landowner had hired workers for his vineyard. Some came in the early morning to work for the whole day for an agreed wage. Three hours later more were hired, then the sixth and the ninth hour. The landowner even hired workers up to the eleventh hour. At the end of the day when they received their wages, they all received the same. This didn't seem fair to the workers that had been there all day, to receive the same as those who had only worked for one hour. To be honest I didn't think it was fair either and couldn't understand why. Until I was in my thirties when the Jesus I thought I knew, became the Jesus I knew in a personal way. I was standing cooking dinner for my family when the Holy Spirit reminded me of this parable. I realised in an instant that what Jesus was saying was that we can come into His kingdom at any stage in our life, whether we accept Him as a child, as a teenager, as a young adult, in middle age or at the eleventh hour of our life. We will all have the same wage (to be part of the kingdom of God) if we answer His call to serve Him. He is the 'Good Shepherd' who continually goes out seeking the lost sheep (Matthew 18:10-14). He brings them home rejoicing, because it is not the Father's will that anyone should perish (Matthew 18:14).

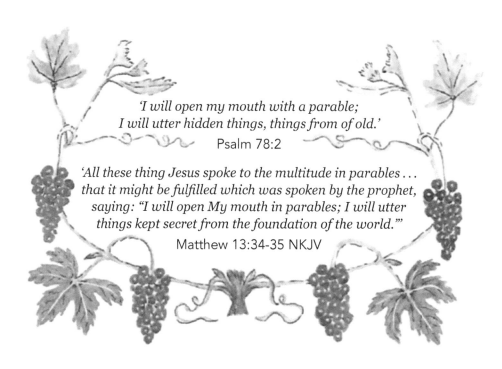

'I will open my mouth with a parable;
I will utter hidden things, things from of old.'
Psalm 78:2

'All these thing Jesus spoke to the multitude in parables . . .
that it might be fulfilled which was spoken by the prophet,
saying: "I will open My mouth in parables; I will utter
things kept secret from the foundation of the world."'
Matthew 13:34-35 NKJV

I AM the

Alpha and Omega

Who was, Who is and Who is to come.

When God called Moses to speak to Pharaoh to secure the freedom of the children of Israel from slavery, He identified Himself as 'I AM WHO I AM' (Exodus 3:14). This was echoed in Isaiah: 'I am the first and I am the last; apart from me there is no God' (Isaiah 44:6).

When the apostle John received a vision of what was to come, God also used the first and the last letters of the Greek alphabet to further explain who He is.

> *"I am the Alpha and the Omega, the Beginning and the End," says the Lord, "who is and who was and who is to come, the Almighty."'*
>
> Revelation 1:8 NKJV

So what does I AM WHO I AM mean? Our minds cannot possibly comprehend all there is to know about our God. But as we move through scripture we see that He reveals Himself in different ways. One of them being in different Hebrew names, which sometimes we lose in translation.

Elohim: Strong and mighty, Creator God (Genesis 1:1-2).

Elohenu Olam: Everlasting God (Genesis 21:33; Psalm 48:14).

El Shaddai: Almighty God, one who is our strength in difficult situations, or at our time of need. 'The LORD appeared to Abram and said to him, "I am Almighty God; walk before Me and be blameless"' (Genesis 17:1).

Jehovah: Often translated as Lord. 'The LORD God' is Jehovah Elohim (Genesis 2:4).

Jehovah Elohim Yeshua: Lord, Mighty God, Saviour, or the Lord of my salvation. David said, 'The LORD is my light and my salvation – whom shall I fear?' (Psalm 27:1). Mary said, 'My spirit rejoices in God my Saviour' (Luke 1:47).

Jehovah Goelekh: Our Lord and Redeemer. 'O LORD my strength and my Redeemer' (Psalm 19:14 NKJV). Psalm 78:35 speaks of 'the Most High God their Redeemer'.

Jehovah Shalom: Lord of our Peace. Gideon built an altar to the Lord and called it 'The LORD Is Peace'(Judges 6:24).

Adonai: Master over all, or my Lord. 'For what god is there in heaven or on earth who can do the deeds and mighty works you do?' (Deuteronomy 3:24). 'Even the winds and the waves obey him!' (Matthew 8:27).

Ruach Elohim: Ruach is the Hebrew word for Spirit, so translates to 'Spirit of God'. The Spirit of God came upon Samuel (1 Samuel 10:10) and on believers (Acts 2). The Holy Spirit is mostly referred to as the 'Spirit of God' but sometimes, as in Philippians 1:19, the 'Spirit of Jesus Christ'. 'And because you are sons, God has sent forth the Spirit of His Son into your hearts' (Galatians 4:6 NKJV).

Kadash: Holy One (Isaiah 40:25). 'Holy, holy, holy is the LORD of hosts' (Isaiah 6:3 NKJV).

The Ancient of Days: Daniel 7:9-28.

Let us look more closely at some of the names of our God.

*'In the beginning God created the heavens
and the earth . . . and the Spirit of God was
hovering over the waters. And God said . . .'*
Genesis 1:1-3

*'You are worthy, our Lord and God, to receive glory and
honour and power, for you created all things, and by
your will they were created and have their being.'*
Revelation 4:11

The first name we look at is **Elohim**, which means 'The strong and mighty, Creator God' or 'God in His fullness'. In Hebrew it is also a plural name, which is interesting when you look at the first chapter in the Bible, which says, 'In the beginning God [**Elohim**] created the heavens and the earth . . . and the Spirit of God [**Ruach Elohim**] was hovering over the waters. And God said, "Let there be light," and there was light' (Genesis 1:1-3). So the creation story goes on, God spoke the **Word** and all things came into being. John starts his gospel with these words:

'In the beginning was the Word [Jesus] and the Word was with God, and the Word was God. He was in the beginning with God. All things were made through Him, and without Him nothing was made.'
John 1:1-3 NKJV

Elohim, the I Am: Just was . . . No one created Him, but He created us.

Elohim divided the light into day and the darkness He called night. He gathered and still gathers the waters into the seas. Even today our water, whether it starts from rain, springs or melt water, flows into streams, then rivers, as it makes its way into the seas. Then dry land appeared, and on the earth grasses, herbs and trees that bear fruit began to grow. He made lights in the heavens; the greater one, the sun, to rule by day and the moon to rule by night.

He set the stars in place, and knows each one by name.
Psalm 147:4

'. . . So that the evening and the morning were the fourth day.'
Genesis 1:14-19 NKJV

This was when time took on the pattern of twenty-four hours per day and seven days made a week. In the time of Jesus, and even today, the Jewish Sabbath is from evening to morning, because at the time of creation darkness turned into light and became day.

Then Elohim spoke the Word and all the sea creatures were created, from the largest whale to the smallest organism. Also every winged bird to fly above the earth and every animal and creeping thing on the earth. Everything that Elohim created, whether it was plants, fish, birds or animals, He created them with the genetics to reproduce 'according to their kinds. And God saw it was good' (Genesis 1:25).

Then He said, 'Let Us make man in Our image' (Genesis 1:26 NKJV; again, plural). He made them male and female, in essence two people, but in marriage they become one (Genesis 2:24).

Then Elohim rested, blessed and sanctified the seventh day.

Mankind had a special place in His heart. He made a garden for them to live in, food for them to eat. He was their **Jehovah Jireh**, their provider. They were allowed to name all that had been created. They had a living relationship with Elohim but they chose to go their own way. They lost their relationship and were banished from the garden. The way back into a living relationship with Elohim was barred. BUT . . .

'God so loved the world . . .'

John 3:16

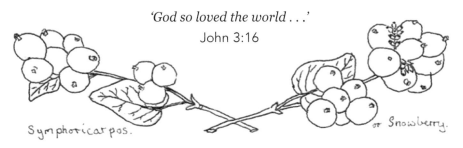

Symphoricarpos. or Snowberry.

'The Word became flesh and made his dwelling among us.
We have seen his glory, the glory of the one and only Son,
who came from the Father, full of grace and truth.'
John 1:14

'Jesus spoke to them . . . saying, "I am the light of the world.
He who follows Me shall not walk in darkness, but have the light of life."'
John 8:12 NKJV

How could man find his way back into a living relationship with his God?

The temple sacrifices offered a way for man to acknowledge and be sorry for his sin, but they did not bring real forgiveness and freedom from guilt. Man could not enter into 'His presence', the veil barred the way. How could this veil be removed?

A prophecy spoken by Isaiah was about to be fulfilled: '"The virgin shall be with child and bear a Son, and they shall call His name **Immanuel**," which is translated, "God with us"' (Isaiah 7:14; Matthew 1:23 NKJV). He lived for a while among us, healing the sick in mind and body and pointing those who would listen back into a living relationship with their God.

—— But, they crucified Him ——

This was when our years were counted from BC Before Christ into AD Anno Domini, which is Latin for 'In the year of our Lord'.

He is our **Jehovah Raphe:** 'Lord our Healer' (Exodus 15:26).

Jehovah Rohi: 'Lord our Shepherd' (Psalm 23). David said, 'The LORD is my shepherd.'

Jehovah Tsidkenu: 'The Lord our Righteousness' (Psalm 4:1). 'God of my righteousness' (NKJV).

> *'He will be called: The LORD our Righteousness.'*
> Jeremiah 23:6 NKJV

The apostle Paul talks much in his letters to the churches about righteousness.

> *'God made him who had no sin to be sin for us, so that in him we might become the righteousness of God.'*
> 2 Corinthians 5:21

When we receive our righteous Lord into our lives, we are saved. And if we continue to live in Him by faith, we are clothed in His righteousness. So open the door of your lives and your hearts to Him.

If you have ever seen Holmen Hunt's remarkable painting 'The Light of the World' you will know it depicts a picture of the risen Christ still with a crown of thorns on His head and a lamp in His hand. He stands knocking on a door that doesn't have a handle, indicating it cannot be opened from the outside, only by the person inside. It represents Revelation 3:20. The church of the Laodiceans thought they were rich and had no need of anything. But, they had left Jesus outside. He says to them and to each one of us:

> *'Here I am! I stand at the door and knock.*
> *If anyone hears my voice and opens the door, I will come in.'*

He is the **Lamb of God**. He became the final sacrifice, to take away the sin of the world. His death removed the veil and opened up the way for us into the 'Holy of Holies'. He rose again and returned to the Father, as our High Priest to intercede for us.

'Alleluia, What a Saviour.'

'...That he gave his one and only Son...'
John 3:16

3rd Arrangement: The Lion and the Lamb 'Who Is To Come'

'A Lion has roared! Who will not fear?
*The Lord G*OD *has spoken!'*
Amos 3:8 NKJV

'Worthy is the Lamb, who was slain, to receive power and wealth
and wisdom and strength and honour and glory and praise!'
Revelation 5:12

'Do not be afraid; I am the First and the Last. I am He who lives,
and was dead, and behold, I am alive forevermore.'
Revelation 1:17-18

After this John saw a door standing open in heaven (Revelation chapter 4). He was called in and before him was the throne of God. A rainbow encircled the throne; day and night the sound of worship filled the air. Twenty-four elders had fallen down in worship. Then John saw the One who sat on the throne, holding a scroll containing prophecies of what was still to come, but no one could open it, until one of the elders said:

'Do not weep. Behold, the Lion of the tribe of Judah, the Root of David,
has prevailed to open the scroll and to loose its seven seals.'
Revelation 5:5 NKJV

Then John looked again and there in the midst of the
elders stood a 'Lamb as though it had been slain'.
Revelation 5:6

Then the elders fell down before the Lamb and sang a new song: 'You are
worthy to take the scroll, and to open its seals; for You were slain, and
have redeemed us to God by Your blood. Out of every tribe and tongue
and people and nation, and have made us kings and priests to our God.'
Revelation 5:9-10 NKJV

Hosea sees the Lion as a judge on the house of Judah and those that reject Him (Hosea 5:14; 11:10; 13:7-8).

Isaiah sees their redeemer return, like a Lion to deliver His people.

'For thus the Lord has spoken to me: "As a lion roars . . .
He will not be afraid of their voice . . .
so the Lord of hosts will come down to fight for Mount Zion.'
Is 31:4

When Jesus was on the earth He showed us more of the character of **Elohim**. He showed us by His love, His compassion, His miracles, His desire to heal and by His words. He said, 'He who hates Me hates My Father also' (John 15:23 NKJV) because

'I and My Father are one.'
John 10:30 NKJV

He tells us God wants us to look on Him as a 'heavenly Father' (Matthew 6:9).

That the very hairs of our head are numbered and we are not to be afraid (Luke 12:7) because at the end of John's vision in Revelation 19 – 22 it tells us that the last spiritual battle will take place and Satan and his armies, whatever form they take, will finally be defeated by the **Word of God** and heaven's armies. He will come riding the White Horse of Victory, He is:

King of kings and Lord of lords
'. . . that whoever believes in him
shall not perish but have eternal life.'
John 3:16

Lion and Lamb

'For God did not send his Son into the world to condemn the world, but to save the world through him. Whoever believes in him is not condemned, but whoever does not believe stands condemned already because they have not believed in the name of God's one and only Son.'

John 3:17-18

Summary

When I see the sky painted in glorious colours of the setting sun, or a delicate snowdrop pushing through the winter frost, giant whales as they jump out of the sea (because of the joy of living) or watch the lifecycle of a butterfly on a nature programme, seeing it change from a caterpillar that crawls on its belly, into a beautiful 'Painted Lady' that can climb to three thousand feet and, assisted by the winds, she flies up to one thousand miles along the Atlantic coast to South Africa. How can a small delicate creature do that? She only has a brain the size of a pinhead, so how does she know the way? So, along with the blackbird sitting on my roof praising his Creator,

I too praise Him and say . . .
'Yes, Lord, your creation is good. Indeed it is Very Good.'

Although the word Trinity doesn't appear in scripture, it's the only way to explain the 'oneness' of the Christian Godhead: 'The Father, Son and Holy Spirit.'

Just as I cannot separate your words from you when you speak to me. I cannot separate the Word from the Father or the Holy Spirit from the Father and the Son. Jesus, **Yeshua**, is the **Word of God**, who in some miraculous way took on human form, so He could become our **Go'el**, our **Kinsman Redeemer**.

Jehovah Goelekh: Lord Redeemer. Isaiah 60:16 says:

'Then you will know that I, the Lord, am your Saviour, your Redeemer.'

To 'redeem' is to repay a ransom, to save or rescue or to make a single payment, to cancel a debt or charge. God had put special provision in the Law for people who had fallen on hard times (Leviticus 25:39-54). A kinsman, a near relative would protect and provide for them. The best way to understand this is to look again at the book of Ruth.

A famine had come upon the land of Judah. Elimelech and his wife Naomi went to live in Moab along with their two sons. But Elimelech died and the two sons married Moabite women named Orpah and Ruth. After about ten years disaster struck again: the two sons died. Naomi decided to go back home to Bethlehem where she still had relatives. She encouraged her daughters-in-law to go back to Moab. Orpah returned to her own people but Ruth chose to stay with Naomi and accepted the God of Judah as her God. They stayed with Boaz, Naomi's kinsman. He protected and provided for them. Even though Ruth was a Gentile, he took care of her also, eventually making her his bride.

Jehovah Elolim Yeshua: (Jesus) is our 'Lord, God of our Salvation'. So like Ruth, place yourself in the hands of your Lord God, Saviour and Redeemer and He will take care of you, and guide you to that 'Holy City' He has prepared for those who love and follow Him (Revelation 21 – 22). He is **Jehovah El Emeth**: 'The Lord God of Truth'.

'God of truth and without injustice' (Deuteronomy 32:4 NKJV)

'Through him all things were made' (John 1:3)

In Him all things hold together (Colossians 1:15-18)

'For all the promises of God in Him are Yes, and . . . Amen'
(2 Corinthians 1:20)

He is the 'Amen', which means 'So be it'.
It's taken from the Hebrew for 'Certainly'.

Thank you, Lord, that you are the Beginning and the End of all things, and you say, 'Yes, I am coming soon,' and we who are redeemed say, 'Amen. Come, Lord Jesus' (Revelation 22:20).

This, this is the God we adore,
Our faithful, unchangeable Friend'
Whose love is as great as His power,
And neither knows measure or end.

'Tis Jesus, the first and the last,
Whose Spirit shall guide us safe home;
We'll praise Him for all that is past,
And trust Him for all that is to come.

Joseph Hart
(1712–1768)

'Trillium'.

Feasts of the Lord
Autumn Feasts

Decorative Dahlia.

It's time to take another look at the seven feasts given to Moses and see what the final three point to in 'His appointed times'. We have seen that the first four have already happened and point to the first coming of Jesus.

First, Passover: representing the shed blood of the Lamb of God.

Second, Unleavened Bread: shows us that He was sinless and we, too, should get rid of all sin in our lives.

Third, Firstfruits: His resurrection, and how He conquered the power of death for the whole human race, so He could say, 'Whoever lives and believes in Me shall never die' (John 11:26 NKJV).

After Jesus returned to His Father, He sent the Helper, the Holy Spirit.

Fourth, Feast of Weeks or Shavuot: tells of the coming of the Holy Spirit to believers on the day we call Pentecost, which took place fifty days after the resurrection.

The final three feasts point to His second coming, a day the prophets call 'The day of the Lord'. Many like Joel, Amos, Jeremiah, etc., speak of it as a time of great trouble, a day of reckoning and judgement. Jesus Himself speaks of it in Matthew 24. We are told not to speculate, just to know the signs and be watchful as no one knows the day or the hour when He will return (v42). Zechariah 14:1-4 tells us that one day, when the nations will gather to do battle against the restored Israel, the Lord will return and 'on that day his feet will stand on the Mount of Olives'.

This is confirmed in the New Testament when the disciples had gone with Jesus after His resurrection to the Mount of Olives. They saw Jesus taken up into heaven, a cloud had hidden Him from their sight. Then two men dressed in white (angels) told them that He would one day return in the same way they saw Him go (Acts 1:11).

Jesus Himself had already told the disciples that He would return.

'If I go and prepare a place for you, I will come again and receive you to Myself; that where I am, there you may be also.'
John 14:3 NKJV

So let us take a brief look at the last three of 'His appointed times'.

Fifth, Feast of Trumpets or Rosh Hashanah.

Sixth, Day of Atonement or Yom Kippur.

Seventh, Feast of Tabernacles or Sukkot.

*'Blow the Trumpet in Zion, consecrate a fast, call a sacred assembly;
gather the people, sanctify the congregation.'*
Joel 2:15-16 NKJV

*'The LORD said to Moses, "Say to the Israelites: 'On the first day of
the seventh month you are to have a day of sabbath rest, a sacred
assembly commemorated with trumpet blasts. Do not do any of
your ordinary work, but present a food offering to the Lord.'"*
Leviticus 23:23-25

'Blow the trumpet in Zion; sound the alarm on my holy hill . . .
for the day of the LORD is coming.'
Joel 2:1

Two kinds of trumpets were used at this time, some were made of silver (Numbers 10:1-10). They were used to gather the people together at the Tabernacle and to blow over their 'peace' and 'burnt' offerings. Also at the beginning of their journeys and when they went to war against their enemies. The other trumpet used was a *Shofar* carved from an animal horn, reminding them of the time God had stepped in and provided Abraham with a ram as a substitute (Genesis 22:1-19). It seems the *Shofar* was used at more specific times when God was speaking or directing them in some way, for example the giving of the Law (Exodus 19:13, 16, 19), the fall of Jericho (Joshua 6:4-6), the return of the Ark (2 Samuel 6:15), and many more instances.

There is not much information in scripture on the Feast of Trumpets, but it's interesting to see that Joel's prophecy in chapter 2 seems to line up with the information we do have in Numbers 29.

Joel 2:1 Speaks of the trumpet being blown in Zion.

Numbers 29:1 (NKJV) 'For you it is a day of blowing the trumpets.'

Joel 2:2 'A day of darkness and gloom.'

Numbers 29:1 It took place in 'the seventh month' and v6 (NKJV) the evening of 'the New Moon' (the darkest time of the year).

Joel 2:12-13 The Lord calls for repentance, before their grain and drink offerings.

Numbers 29:6 Likewise, with the burnt offering and the grain offering.

The Feast of Trumpets fell on the first day of the seventh month of the Hebrew calendar (September/October). It would coincide with the New Moon and the final harvest of the year. Since the destruction of the temple in AD 70, sacrificial offerings could no longer take place. So those ten days were looked on as a time for contemplation and repentance of any sin or unbelief and to remember the sovereignty of their God, before the 'Day of the Lord' comes (Joel 2:30-32).

To judge the nations and to save those who call on His name.
They were referred to as the 'Days of AWE'.

'Let all the earth fear the Lord; let all the inhabitants of the world stand in awe of Him.'
Psalm 33:8 NKJV

'Then the Lord will appear over them . . .
The Sovereign Lord will sound the trumpet . . .
The Lord their God will save his people on
that day as a shepherd saves his flock.'
Zechariah 9:14-16

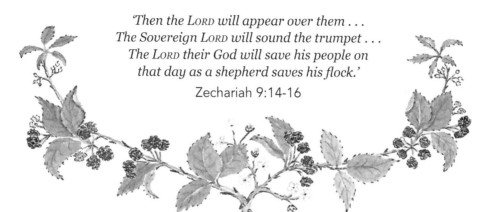

2nd Arrangement: The Day of Atonement or Yom Kippur

'On the tenth day of this seventh month you shall have a holy convocation. You shall afflict your souls; you shall not do any work.'
Numbers 29:7 NKJV

'The priests entered regularly into the outer room to carry on their ministry. But only the high priest entered the inner room, and that only once a year, and never without blood, which he offered for himself and for the sins the people had committed in ignorance.'
Hebrews 9:6-7

Following on from the Feast of Trumpets, on the tenth day of the seventh month comes the Day of Atonement. The most important day of the Hebrew calendar when the High Priest (Aaron) would come and make atonement for himself, the priesthood and the people. It is the only day of the year that he was allowed to go beyond the veil into the 'Holy of Holies' to offer the blood sacrifice into the very presence of God and to sprinkle it on the mercy seat. Leviticus 16 gives us a detailed account of the Day of Atonement. The High Priest would:

1. Bring a bull as a sin offering for himself and the other priests (vs3, 6, 11).
2. Go inside the veil, taking coals from the altar of sacrifice to burn sweet incense before the Lord. He then takes some of the blood from the bull to sprinkle on the ground and the mercy seat, which is placed on top of the Ark of the Covenant (vs12-14).
3. He also takes two identical goats (vs7-10): one to kill as a sin offering for the people (vs15-16), then on the other one, the 'scapegoat', he places his hands on its head and confesses the people's sins. The scapegoat is then released into the wilderness, taking the sins of the people with it, never to return (vs20-22).
4. They continually make sure their body is washed and their clothing clean before and during the temple service (vs4, 23-24, 28).

The first time we visited Israel we had a Jewish guide who had grown up in America, but had returned to live in her homeland. Talking to her one day I said, 'As Christians we believe that Jesus was the Lamb of God, who died to pay the price for our sin. But as the Jews can no longer sacrifice, how can those who don't believe in Jesus find forgiveness for their sin?' She replied, 'Yom Kippur is the day in Israel when everything stops. No work is done. They spend their time thinking over the past year and any sin they have committed in thought, word or deed. If they have offended anyone they go to that person to put it right. It is their most sacred day of the year when they truly come before their God to atone for their sin.' Apparently, a rabbi who lived at the time of the destruction of the temple, talked afterwards that loving kindness was the way they should go, which is not wrong in itself. Jesus also said one of the greatest ways we should live is to 'love one another', but we must not miss the greatest gift of love that anyone can give, which was when God gave His Son to be sin for us. Romans 5:8 explains this more fully.

'While we were sinners, Christ died for us.'
'Not with the blood of goats and calves, but with His own blood He entered the Most Holy Place once for all, having obtained eternal redemption.'
Hebrews 9:12 NKJV

3rd Arrangement: The Feast of Tabernacles or Sukkot

*'Celebrate the Festival of Tabernacles for seven days after you have gathered the produce of your threshing-floor and your winepress. Be joyful at your festival . . . For the L*ORD *your God will bless you in all your harvest and in all the work of your hands, and your joy will be complete.'*
Deuteronomy 16:13-15

*'And it shall come to pass that everyone who is left of all the nations which came against Jerusalem shall go up from year to year to worship the King, the L*ORD *of hosts, and to keep the Feast of the Tabernacles.'*
Zechariah 14:16 NKJV

The Feast of Tabernacles or Sukkot is the most joyful of all the feasts as it is a celebration of the presence of God with the Jews when they were in the wilderness. The Hebrew word Sukkot means 'booths', temporary huts or shelters, which they made out of leafy plants, date palms, willow and citrus trees. As well as a thanksgiving for God's past provision, they also look forward to their coming Messiah.

The Feast follows on directly after the Day of Atonement, on the fifteenth day of the seventh month. It starts and ends with a Sabbath. All the day's activities are listed in Numbers 29:12-40. They had regular sin offerings, burnt offerings, grain and drink offerings, etc. They were to live in booths for seven days (Leviticus 23:42). The Tabernacle would be filled with the sweet smell of incense. Olives would be crushed to make oil, so the lamps in the Tabernacle and later in the Temple could burn continuously throughout the festival (Leviticus 24:1-4).

As with all the feasts, it follows the pattern of the harvests. This one falls at the time of the final harvest of the year (the wheat), and as such it is sometimes also referred to as 'The Feast of Ingathering'.

> *'Celebrate the Festival of Ingathering at the end of the year,*
> *when you gather in your crops from the field.'*
>
> Exodos 23:16b

As there is normally no rain in Israel over the summer, they rely greatly on the rains that come in the autumn and winter months, to provide enough water for next year's harvest. So a celebration of water is also observed. Each day the priests would take a golden pitcher to the Pool of Siloam to collect some water. He takes it back to the Temple and pours it out on the altar as a thank offering, while the people sang the song of praise from Isaiah 12:

> *'With joy you will draw water from the wells of salvation.'*
>
> v3

Many years later scripture tells us that a man called Jesus had joined the crowds at the Feast of Tabernacles. He stood up and cried out saying:

> *'If anyone thirsts, let him come to Me and drink. He who believes in Me,*
> *as Scripture has said, out of his heart will flow rivers of living water.'*
>
> John 7:37-39 NKJV

Abutilons.

Fritillaria imperiallis.
'Crown Imperial'.

Jesus links Himself to the Feasts, because He is the pure water of life that was poured out for us. He is both the sin offering whose blood was shed for us, and He is the scapegoat, who has taken our sins far away from us. The sprinkling of His blood has cleansed every part of our life. He has washed us and made us clean. He is our High Priest who has entered the Most Holy Place and He stands before the throne of the Most High God as a mediator of the new covenant that God had given to Jeremiah many years before:

> *'I will put my law in their minds and write it on their hearts.*
> *I will be their God, and they will be my people.'*
> Jeremiah 31:33-34

It's more than two thousand years since God started to put His plan for our redemption into action through the life, death and resurrection of our Lord and Saviour.

The prophets and Jesus Himself spoke many times of His return. In Matthew 24 – 25 Jesus tells His disciples what will happen in the world. There are many things prophesied to take place, but let us just look at three, which I would class as the main ones:

1. **The times of the Gentiles.**
    After the destruction of the temple in AD 70 and the people were displaced to all parts of the world (hence the word Diaspora), the disciples and believers took the message with them (Luke 21:20-24): '. . . And they will fall by the edge of the sword, and be led away captive into all the nations. And Jerusalem will be trampled by Gentiles until the times of the Gentiles are fulfilled' (v24 NKJV).

2. **The sons of Jacob (Israel) will return to the land God gave them.**
    'This is what the Sovereign LORD says : I will gather you from the nations and bring you back from the countries where you have been scattered, and I will give you back the land of Israel again' (Ezekiel 11:17).

3. **The veil will be removed when they turn to the Lord** (2 Corinthians 3:13-16).
    Zechariah 12:10 tells us they will recognise Him as Messiah and mourn. 'And I will pour on the house of David and the inhabitants of Jerusalem the Spirit of grace and supplication; then they will look on Me whom they pierced. Yes, they will mourn for Him as one mourns for his only son' (NKJV). And then they will say:

'Blessed is he who comes in the name of the Lord.'
Matthew 23:39

The Autumn Feasts guide us through what will take place in the 'Final Ingathering'

Bougainvillea.

Feast of Trumpets: Jesus said, 'He will send his angels with a loud trumpet call, and they will gather his elect from the four winds, from one end of the heavens to the other' (Matthew 24:31). Paul says in 1 Thessalonians 4:13-18 that the sound of the *Shofar* will herald the coming of the Lord. That the Lord Himself will come down from heaven with a loud command, with the voice of an archangel and with the trumpet call of God. The dead in Christ will rise first, after which those who are still alive will be caught up to meet the Lord. And we will be with Him forever.

Paul explains in 1 Corinthians 15:42-44 that we will have a new and glorious body, as a body sown in corruption will be raised in corruption; sown in dishonour, raised in glory; sown in weakness, raised in power; sown a natural body, raised a spiritual body.

'In a moment, in a twinkling of an eye, at the last trumpet . . .
we shall be changed.'
v52 NKJV

'Death is swallowed up in victory.'
v54 NKJV

He gives the victory to those who have repented, believed and received Jesus into their lives, and know that the risen Christ is their hope and they are awaiting His return.

'Blessed are all those who put their trust in Him.'
Psalm 2:12 NKJV

You may be thinking this was all prophesied thousands of years ago, so how can we believe it will happen? I would say to you, all the other prophecies about Jesus have come true with such accuracy, so why should we not believe these? Peter had to answer questions and doubts about the second coming of Jesus. He said,

'Do not forget this one thing, dear friends: with the Lord a day is like a thousand years, and a thousand years are like a day. The Lord is not slow in keeping his promise, as some understand slowness. Instead he is patient with you, not wanting anyone to perish, but everyone to come to repentance. But the day of the Lord will come.

2 Peter 3:8-1

So ... 'Seek the LORD while he may be found.'

Isaiah 55:6

'Truly, these times of ignorance God overlooked, but now commands all men everywhere to repent, because He has appointed a day on which He will judge the world in righteousness.'

Acts 17:30-31 NKJV

Which brings us to **The Day of Atonement**.

Over the years traditions and the way we worship change but one thing never changes: the need to repent. During the Feast of Yom Kippur the book of Jonah is read to remind the people of the need to repent and return to the Lord because they had gone their own way. It was the main criteria as John the Baptist prepared the way for the coming Saviour (Matthew 3:2). Matthew goes on to tell us that when John was put in prison, Jesus began His ministry by saying to the people:

'Repent, for the kingdom of heaven is at hand.'

Matthew 4:17 NKJV

In Matthew 13, in the form of parables, Jesus tells us He will judge all people (vs25-51) and the nations (Matthew 25:31-46).

'The Father judges no one, but has entrusted all judgment to the Son' (John 5:22).

Sacrifice for sin goes back to the time of Adam and Eve, when God sacrificed an animal to 'cover' their sin. Over the years they have been used for thanksgiving, atonement and when a new covenant was put in place. The laws concerning the offerings are found in Leviticus chapters 1 to 7:

Burnt Offerings: Signify the complete sacrifice and surrender to the Father's will by Jesus. Also our commitment to Him should be total.

Meal Offering: Thanksgiving to God for our physical and spiritual food.

Peace Offering: Also thanksgiving for our heavenly food and to find peace with our God. Jesus said, 'My peace I give you' (John 14:27) and

'In me you may have peace.'
John 16:33

Sin Offering: For our sin He became sin, to die in our place and for the whole of mankind (2 Corinthians 5:21).

Trespass Offering: For the sins we have committed against God and our fellow man. All these offerings would take place on the Day of Atonement, but, it was only a shadow of the things to come.

As Isaiah foretold and the New Testament confirms, one day approximately eight hundred years later, God sent His Son to live among us.

'He [was] despised and rejected . . . a man of sorrows . . . we esteemed him not' (Isaiah 53:3 KJV).

'Though the world was made through him, the world did not recognise him' (John 1:10).

'He took up our pain and bore our suffering' (Isaiah 53:4).

'"He himself bore our sins" in his body on the cross, so that we might die to sins' (1 Peter 2:24).

'He was pierced for our transgressions, he was crushed for our iniquities' (Isaiah 53:5).

'Christ was sacrificed once to take away the sins of many' (Hebrews 9:28).

'The punishment that brought us peace was on him, and by his wounds we are healed' (Isaiah 53:5).

He will appear a second time. Not to bear sin,
but to bring salvation to those who are waiting for Him.

Dear Friends, the sacrifices are no longer required because He has paid the whole price for our redemption. All we have to do is Repent, Believe and Receive our wonderful Lord and Saviour into our lives, with a heart of thanksgiving and love, in order to know and walk with our God once more.

That's exactly what the **Feast of Tabernacles** is all about as the Jews remember the time God was with them in the wilderness, how He fed them and gave them fresh water springing from the rock. He led them in the day by a pillar of cloud to protect them from the heat of the sun, and at night by a pillar of fire, which also gave them warmth in the cold night air. That 'glory' or presence of the Lord is sometimes referred to as 'Shekinah glory'. It also filled the Temple built by Solomon when the Ark of the Covenant was brought there, and was mentioned by Zechariah after the rebuilding of Jerusalem.

> *"'For I," says the LORD, "will be a wall of fire all around her,*
> *and I will be the glory in her midst."'*
> Zechariah 2:5 NKJV

Isaiah also speaks of this light.

> *'The sun shall no longer be your light . . . nor the moon . . . But the*
> *LORD will be to you an everlasting light, and your God your glory.'*
> Isaiah 60:19 NKJV

In Revelation 19:11-13 John saw,

> *'Heaven standing open and there before me a white horse, whose rider*
> *is called Faithful and True . . . On his head are many crowns . . . He is*
> *dressed in a robe dipped in blood, and his name is the Word of God.'*

The Bible completes a full circle when the enemy of our souls is finally defeated and God will once again live among His people. Not in a garden this time but in His 'Holy City – The New Jerusalem' (Revelation chapters 21 – 22).

> *'I saw a new heaven and a new earth . . . I heard a loud voice*
> *from heaven saying, "Behold, the tabernacle of God is with*
> *men, and He will dwell with them, and they shall be His*
> *people. God Himself will be with them and be their God."'*
> Revelation 21:1-3 NKJV

There will be no more death, sorrow or pain (v4).

The city has no need of the sun or moon for the glory of God gives it light, and the Lamb is its lamp, and the nations will walk in its light. The river of life runs through it, flowing from the throne of God and the Tree of Life brings healing for those whose names are found written in the book of life.
Revelation 22:1-2

'The Spirit and the bride say, "Come!" And let the one who hears say, "Come!" Let the one who is thirsty come; and let the one who wishes take the free gift of the water of life.'
Revelation 22:17

'He who testifies to these things says, "Yes, I am coming soon."'
Revelation 22:20

'Amen. Come, Lord Jesus!'

End Note

The Old and the New Testaments come together in Him.
The old and the new covenants are signed and sealed in Him.
The prophecies and promises are fulfilled in Him.
The Feasts point to Him.
He is our Jubilee.

As well as the yearly pattern of months that lead to the harvest, as shown in the Feasts, there is also a pattern of years. For instance, we have six days to work and one day of rest. In Leviticus 25:1-7 we find the same applied to the years as they were to work their land for six years and let it rest on the seventh year.

Just as God poured out His Spirit on believers fifty days after the resurrection, so the years of Jubilee will occur on the fiftieth year. The timing of this has been lost over the years, but verse nine goes on to say:

'Then you shall cause the trumpet of the Jubilee to sound on the tenth day of the seventh month; on the Day of Atonement.'

When that trumpet sounds liberty is proclaimed throughout the land, slaves are set free, debts cancelled, property and land is returned to its rightful owners, everything will be restored.

Ezekiel 37 points to Israel being restored when God shows him the valley of dry bones. Verses 12-14 say He will take them back to the land of Israel. God spoke to him again in verses 15-22, telling him to take two sticks and write on one 'Israel' and the other 'Judah', and hold them together in his hand. They represented the prophecies and the promise that God would make them one nation again. That He would cleanse them from their sin and He would make an everlasting 'Covenant of Peace' with them. He will 'Tabernacle' with them. He will be their God and they will be His people.

The prophecies mentioned earlier are being fulfilled.

1. Jerusalem has been trampled on by other nations for about two thousand years. From the time of the Roman occupation through to 1917 when the British troops overcame the Turks. (A great-uncle of mine died in that battle. He was buried in Gaza.)

2. In 1948 they were officially one nation again when they were given their land back. It has not been without problems, but since then they have been returning in ever-increasing numbers. Christians have been supporting them. In 1980 the International Christian

Embassy Jerusalem was formed. They and other Christian organisations have all played a part in helping them return and settle back in the land God gave Abraham via Jacob's sons thousands of years ago.

3. The veil is being removed. More and more Jews are coming to see that Jesus is their Messiah.

The Fig Tree is budding again. Jesus said,

> *'Now learn this lesson from the fig-tree: as soon as its twigs become tender and its leaves come out, you know that summer is near.'*

Matthew 24:32-33

The Olive Tree will be pruned and the Gentiles will be grafted in, and

Together they share the root.

The Feasts of the Lord are being fulfilled in **His Appointed Times.** There is bread for all in **Joseph's Storehouse,** and that spring of Living Water will continue to flow from the Rock. As we clothe ourselves in the **Armour of His Word**

We must continue to pray for His harvest and love one another, as He helps and guides us by **His grace** through the **Wilderness Years** into **His heavenly kingdom.**

Rosa Rubrifolia.

Jesus looked towards heaven and prayed that all His disciples, both Jew and Gentile, become one (John 17).

'Father, the hour has come. Glorify your Son, that your Son may glorify you. For you granted him authority over all people that he might give eternal life to all those you have given him. Now this is eternal life: that they know you, the only true God, and Jesus Christ, whom you have sent . . . Now, Father, glorify me in your presence with the glory I had with you before the world began. I have revealed you to those whom you gave me out of the world. They were yours; you gave them to me and they have obeyed your word . . . For I gave them the words you gave me and they accepted them. They knew with certainty that I came from you, and they believed that you sent me. I pray for them.'

vs1-9

'My prayer is not for them alone. I pray also for those who will believe in me through their message, that all of them may be one, Father, just as you are in me and I am in you. May they also be in us so that the world may believe that you have sent me . . . So that they may be brought to complete unity. Then the world will know that you sent me and have loved them even as you have loved me. Father, I want those you have given me to be with me where I am , and to see my glory, the glory you have given me because you loved me before the creation of the world. Righteous Father, though the world does not know you, I know you, and they know you have sent me. I have made you known to them, and will continue to make you known in order that the love you have for me may be in them and that I myself may be in them.'

vs20-26